Breaking All The Rules

An Ancient Framework for Modern Faith

Kristian A. Smith

Breaking All The Rules: An Ancient Framework for Modern Faith
ISBN: Softcover 978-1-951472-62-7

www.parsonsporch.com

Breaking All The Rules

Dedication

This book is dedicated to my late father, Willie James Smith Sr. I exist because of you. I am who I am because of you. I do what I do because of you. Your spirit still lives in me. Your body may not be here, but your spirit will never die. I love you, Pops.

Acknowledgements

This entire project has been a communal effort, including the people that shared in raising me like my mom, Toni Smith, my God-mom, Linda Daniels, my God-sister, Quieter Russ, my siblings Will and Kelli, my nieces, my nephew, my grandparents, uncles, aunties and cousins on the Robinson side and Smith side of my family.

This effort also includes those whose relationships continue to sustain me daily like my beautiful wife and life partner, Pamela Merritt. I don't know if anyone believes in me like Pamela does and it means the world to me. My friends who help me work through life and the process of writing include Arthur Humphrey, Myron Randall, Tiger Gibson, Stephen Thurston Jr., Dr. Greg Deloach, Dr. Geneva Gray, Grayson Hester, and Kervance D. Ross.

To my present and former pastors who have helped shape my ministry over the years: My late uncle, Pastor Gordon Humphrey Jr., my spiritual father, Pastor T.C. Johnson (aka Pop), Bishop Eric Hutton, Dr. E. Dewey Smith, and Pastor Spencer O'Neal.

To the entire faculty and staff of McAfee School of Theology at Mercer University, thank you for equipping me with the tools to do this meaningful work. Also to my beloved alma mater, Alabama A&M University: Blessed be thy name. Long live thy fame.

And last but not least to my church, The Faith Community. Thank you for trusting my leadership as we take this faith journey together. We are changing the world.

Contents

Foreword

Reginald Wayne Sharpe, Jr.

As a young, precocious student at Morehouse College majoring in Religion, I recall sitting in Introduction to Theology class taught by Dr. Aaron L. Parker. This class made an unerasable impact in my life because for the first time, I was introduced to the concept that wrestling with one's faith is a noble undertaking. That was unsettling and unnerving considering all of my life, I was comfortable rehearsing what pastors and Sunday School teachers had taught me. Dr. Parker, who earned a PhD in Systematic Theology shared two ideas that have greatly contributed to my intellectual and spiritual flowering.

First, Parker introduced our class to a book entitled How To Think Theologically. He used this book to introduce the notion of embedded theology and deliberative theology. Embedded theology are all of the theological convictions that have been passed to us from family, spiritual leaders, and culture. Typically, embedded theology isn't harmful until it is and we can't disconnect from it logically because we are so tied to it emotionally. For instance, if I were to say to anyone who grew up in the Black church context, "God is good", it would not surprise me if someone responds, "all the time." It's embedded in us. Some statements we don't question or challenge; we simply accept it.

Then there is deliberative theology. The root word is deliberate. When one deliberates, she or he thinks about a thought carefully and deeply. Deliberative theology invites us to ask questions, ponder ideas, rethink cliches, discard certain opinions or explain why we hold so tightly to particular convictions. Now, when someone says, "God is good", there have been times along my journey that I respond by adding, "Yes, God is God." For me, goodness is God's essence. However, a mother who has to bury her child one week after giving birth to that child may need space to wrestle with the goodness of God juxtaposed to her suffering and grief. Deliberative theology grants us space and grace to question and dialogue about the things of God. Sometimes we do not need "a sermon or a lecture" we need to meditate, listen, and listen again.

The second deposit Dr. Parker made into the life of my mind was a quote from Paul Tillich. In Tillich's tome, Systematic Theology Volume I, he argues, "A theological system is supposed to satisfy two basic needs: the statement of the truth of the Christian message and the interpretation of this truth for every new generation." This quote helped me understand that every responsible theologian, must hold the truth of God's message while making it relevant for the social location and cultural context of the listeners she or he seeks to reach. Everyone who speaks about God is a theologian. The problem is everyone is not responsible.

I believe, what Kristian A. Smith has done in this groundbreaking work offers each of us space to deliberate and helps us interpret the Christian message for this generation. It's time for people to stop cancelling other people because they dare to think differently. Smith pushes back on some ancient doctrines. It is important for all of us to learn that "doctrine" and "divine" are not synonyms. A doctrine is a set of beliefs that a group or institution in power decides everyone should agree on and repeat. Have we considered that even Jesus pushed back from the set Jewish doctrines of his day? Every time Jesus said, "Ye have heard it was said by them of old time…But I say unto you…" (Matthew 5:21-22) Jesus was trying to interpret a truth for a new generation. Smith is a follower of Jesus and his thought-provoking work challenges us to hear the voice of God in a post-modern world.

There is a hymn that I would hear sung in my home church and I've discovered very few people believe the lyrics. The hymn is called, A Charge To Keep I Have and it reads:

A charge to keep I have,
A God to glorify
A never-dying soul to save
And fit it for the sky.
To serve this present age,
My calling to fulfill:
Oh, may it all my pow'rs engage
To do my Master's will.

In this book, Smith's heart is to serve this present age. Smith welcomes us into an unfamiliar sanctuary—a space where all of the pews are in the pulpit. No one will stand to preach today. Both, preacher, and people, are invited to sit beside each other to converse and listen, and that's all. Please remember as you sit in this space reading this book, if you know everything then you don't need faith, and if you have faith you don't need to know everything.

Finally, whenever someone says something new or does something new, our first "knee-jerk" reaction is to reject it, resent it, or emotively respond to it. I pray this book ignites conversations without feeling the need to lead crucifixions. In the words of Dr. Howard-John Wesley, "My job is not to make you think like me, my job is to make you think." Kristian Smith makes us think. Let's think together and may we all leave this book knowing, both, God is good and God is God. Let the adventure begin…

Reginald Wayne Sharpe Jr.

Chapter 1

Gaping Holes

Where do I begin? This book has been a few years in the making. I have had people admonish me and others chastise me for waiting so long to write. So here I am in the midst of a pandemic coupled with the most severe race riots our country has seen in decades, writing about theology.

How did I get here? I am a preacher's kid (PK). I grew up in the National Baptist Convention. (Don't ask me which one. There are too many versions for me to keep track.) My father was a Mississippi native who married my Texas-born mother in 1978. They moved to The Bay Area of California; in 1984, they gave birth to me in Oakland. I am a fifth-generation preacher. I would say "Baptist" preacher, but I'm not sure if that category fits me anymore. What follows on the pages of this book may suggest that I don't cleanly fit into any denominational category.

My parents raised me to think for myself. My dad used to require me to "state my case" when I had a special request. I had to be able to logically explain why my request should be granted. This is the reason my wife, Pamela, sometimes says I should have become a courtroom litigator. I have been arguing cases since I can remember. For instance, consider this childhood episode: I had a midnight curfew in high school. My best friend had no curfew. So we would strategize how to build an argument to convince my parents to let me spend the night at his house on the weekends we wanted to go to the teen club or house parties. One condition I knew I had to meet was to be on the drum set at the church on Sunday morning for 7:30 service, ready to play. I spent many sleep-deprived mornings in church during my high school years. But hey, that's the price a PK pays to hang out with our friends.

My dad was also rather disruptive, which ties into how he taught me to think for myself. I've been exposed to women preachers for as long as I can remember. I didn't know that my dad was being disruptive in his denomination by licensing and ordaining women preachers back in the late 80's and early 90's. It was commonplace for me. It didn't come full circle for me until 25 years later when I was invited to preach at a church in The Bay Area in 2015. As is my normal routine, I sat in the pastor's office to clear my thoughts and pray before going out to the sanctuary for worship. When the pastor came to the office to lead me to the sanctuary, he stopped me and said, "Before we go out here, I need to warn you that there are women in the pulpit." I had the most perplexed look on my face as I responded, "Ok. That's great. Why are you telling me this?" He replied, "Well I just like to put it out there. A lot of the pastors in this area don't believe in women preachers and some of them have cut off fellowship with me because I have women preachers in my church." At that moment, I realized just how disruptive my dad had been 25 years earlier. And I actually wore it as a badge of honor.

My parents also raised me to honor and respect other people, no matter their lot in life, whether it was the trans sex worker who worked the corner across the street from the church or the president of the convention. I have a heart for people because my parents modeled what that looked like for me. Looking back, I see how my father's theological framework sometimes led him to make ill-informed statements about people, but I know his heart. I believe if he were alive today, we would be having some intense and lively conversations about the contents of this book. Even if he would not ultimately agree with my conclusions, he would have to appreciate the logic of it all; that is, after all, who he raised me to be.

My dad was my favorite preacher, but he didn't try to force preaching on me as a vocation. I admired and imitated preachers growing up, but that was not my career aspiration. I played football, studied telecommunications and business administration at Alabama Agricultural & Mechanical University in Normal, Alabama founded by William Hooper Council in 1875 (I love my alma mater, in case you couldn't tell.) My career aspirations were to be a corporate executive. I am equally as committed to being effective in the marketplace as I am to being faithful in ministry. I am writing this book as I sit in the clothing studio of P-Squared Custom Clothiers, my family-owned custom clothing and wardrobe consulting firm. As much as I love the church, I see God in all aspects of society including, but not limited to, business, nature, and sports. My theology is influenced by this worldview.

And speaking of theology, I studied it formally at Mercer University's McAfee School of Theology in Atlanta. It was during my time at McAfee that I was exposed to some inconsistencies in my theology. I can't shake how often Dr. Lloyd Allen, my church history professor, would drop some earth-shattering knowledge on us and then say, "Mama n' them never told you that, huh?" I can't shake the first time Dr. Dave Garber, my Old Testament professor, exposed me to a Native American reading of the story of Joshua and the Battle of Jericho. I don't have the words to explain how it felt to hear a Native American say they identify with the non-aggressive people inside the walls of Jericho whose city was besieged by the Israelites. Not to mention, Dave told the class that he's not really a fan of King David in the Old Testament (Dave is a member of my church now, so I have permission to call him by his first name.) But seriously…

who doesn't like King David? I mean, he was a man after God's own heart! Aren't we *required* to like King David?

But, hey, my parents taught me to think for myself, so my thought was, "Let's see where this seminary thing goes." In the proverbial words of my elders, I could just eat the meat and leave the bone. My seminary journey revealed to me that my embedded theology contained a lot of bones. By "embedded theology" I mean the perspective of God my faith tradition instilled in me during my developmental years, which shaped my worldview. That's not to say that my embedded theology wasn't useful. I came to know God using my embedded theology. I just didn't know how many bones were mixed in with the meat until someone showed me that there are other perspectives to the story.

I am very careful to not always tell people to think outside the box. That can be dangerous. There are some valuable lessons inside of our boxes. I met God inside a box of male-dominated, patriarchal, National Baptist church life and theology. That box had and still has all types of flaws, but I met God there. God is inside the box. The problem is when we limit God to our box. God isn't relegated to the box where we met God. God is in my box. God is in my neighbor's box. God is also outside of all of our boxes. So, by all means, think outside the box. But don't completely discard the good things you learned about God in the box where you met God.

Nonetheless, I hit a wall in my faith journey as I was further educated about my faith tradition. I discovered that there were some gaping holes in my theological framework that I never noticed, primarily because of my privilege. I am a black, heterosexual, cisgender, able-bodied male who was raised in the black Baptist church, one of the few places in this country where black men have authority. (Cisgender basically means that my gender identity matches the sex I was assigned at birth. I was assigned male at birth based on my genitalia and I identify as male. The alternative to cisgender is transgender.) Nothing about my theology was oppressive to me, except the shame and stigma surrounding sex in general. Most of us have dealt with that to some degree (another book for another day).

Yes, the perverted brand of Christianity that white colonizers handed to my African ancestors is harmful in every way. Their sanitized version of Jesus which they used to pacify slaves was diabolical. But that isn't the type of Christianity I practiced growing up. I never had pictures of White Jesus in my home. My parents always pointed out to me that the people of the Bible were people of color. I'll never forget my dad telling me at a young age that Jesus looked more like us than the guy in the framed pictures that hang on many black people's living room walls, in between Martin Luther King Jr. and John F. Kennedy. Here was his rationale: In Matthew 2:13 the angel of the Lord tells Joseph that he must flee to Egypt to hide because Herod is looking for Jesus so he can kill him. Why would God tell a blonde-haired, blue-eyed pale-skinned person to hide out in an African nation? Joseph's family would have stuck out like a sunburnt thumb. I could go much further into this topic about how black people think Christianity is "the white man's religion," but that is not my assignment in this book. Let me stay on task.

I said all of that to say that I grew up in a faith tradition that was very affirming of who I am as a black man with the attributes I listed above. Once I was removed from my theological echo chamber and placed in a setting with a more diverse group of people of faith, I was able to hear much more clearly the cries of my neighbors who did not experience the privilege I did in my tradition. I was able to clearly hear the cries of women who were marginalized by my faith tradition. I was able to hear the cries of LGBT(Q+)

people who had been oppressed and ostracized by the very faith tradition that had formed and shaped me. And by diverse, I don't simply mean racial or ethnic diversity. Too often that's the only thing that comes to mind when we say "diverse." Sure, I did experience more racial and ethnic diversity in my theological education setting. But just as important, I encountered cultural and theological diversity. I studied alongside Africans who looked like me but had a drastically different cultural lens than I did. I studied alongside black women who looked like me but had a different theological lens than I did.

This forced me to come to grips with the reality that I was conditioned to use my critical thought in every aspect of my life except for my theology. I wasn't taught to critically question what I was taught in church. I was taught to accept it and adjust to it. My formal theological education didn't tell me what to think. It gave me permission to question. One of the hallmarks of my ministry is that my aim is not to provide answers for your questions. I want to provide questions for your answers. My theological education equipped me with the tools to carry out my questioning experiment. That experiment is what led to the curation of Greatest Commandment Theology. I'm careful not to refer to myself as the creator of Greatest Commandment Theology because I don't think I created anything. I think I just connected the dots that were already there. That's what it means to curate something. A curator organizes and connects dots. I liken it to the work I do as a clothier and stylist. I design clothes and shoes using fabrics, threads, buttons, and other materials that already exist. Then I organize the various garments and accessories to create an aesthetically pleasing presentation. I have the most fun when I encounter a client who doesn't have the greatest sense of style, but they know they want to look better. That's when my creative juices really get flowing. Greatest Commandment Theology is my spiritual style presentation.

And it all started with me recognizing that my personal theological style had some deficiencies that needed to be addressed. What are those deficiencies, you may ask? That's a great question. Thanks for asking. Turn the page and let's explore them together.

Chapter 2

Navigating Biblical Authority

My Divorce

I endured a pretty ugly divorce from my first wife when I was about 26. I'll spare you the details because you probably wouldn't believe me if I told you the truth. Maybe I'll write a fiction novel one day and sell the rights to a screenwriter because that story is Sundance-Film-Festival worthy. Nonetheless, I grew up believing that divorce was wrong. Again, my father was my pastor, and he didn't condemn divorcees. How could he? He divorced my older brother's mom before he married my mom and gave birth to my big sister and me. I really shouldn't say "how could he?" A lot of people condemn and chastise others for the very things they have done and continue to do. But that wasn't my dad's thing. He tried to be as rational as possible. The message I received about divorce being wrong and sinful was rooted in the theology of my faith tradition, not my dad's preaching and teaching. Nonetheless, I felt a significant level of guilt and anxiety when I decided to initiate my divorce because of irreconcilable differences.

What surprised me was how the spiritual leaders in my life responded. Unfortunately, my father died before I initiated the divorce, so I couldn't process this situation with his guidance. But thank God I was surrounded with some other people who encouraged me through the journey. I expected to hear my spiritual advisers and confidants tell me that I needed to stick it out and that I made a vow before God; that those vows are binding for better or for worse, til death do us part. Oddly enough I only received those messages from my ex-wife's family as they campaigned for me to stay in the marriage.

My spiritual advisers on the other hand… well, let's just say they were very supportive of my decision. I was told, "Boy, you better get the hell out of there!" When I told one of my spiritual advisers of my decision to get a divorce, his response was, "Congratulations." I can't tell you how encouraging and disconcerting this was for me. It was encouraging because I was in an unhealthy relationship that was draining the life out of me. It was disconcerting because the advice I received did not line up with the Rule-Keeping Theology I was raised to practice.

Doctrine vs. Bible

My embedded theology focused much more on rule-keeping. I grew up with the idea that our theological notion of being "set apart" was defined by the number of rules we could keep. Good Christians were people who do the following:

- Consistently pay their tithes.
- Pray every day
- Read the entire Bible literally
- Go to church every Sunday.
    - The best Christians also go to Bible Study on Wednesdays.
        - And if Christians want extra credit in heaven, they are also in at least one other ministry that requires them to be at the church an additional day of the week.

Good Christians don't do the following:

- Don't have sex unless they are married.

- Don't even talk about sex unless they are telling someone not to have sex unless they are married.

- Don't go to the nightclub.

- Don't go to parties.

- Don't use profanity.

- Don't wear revealing clothing.

- Don't listen to secular music.

- Don't get a divorce.

- Don't drink liquor.

The lists go on and on and on. The church and denomination you are a part of determines what makes the list and what is highly prioritized on said list. My wife grew up in a Pentecostal faith tradition where playing cards and going to the movie theater also appear on the list of "don'ts." But we Baptists are much more worldly than many of our Pentecostal counterparts.

Regardless of our denomination, the reality for many of us is that our status as a "good Christian" is tied to rule-keeping. So, for me to break the divorce rule and be praised by the people who raised me in this tradition was off-putting. I figured they would at least say, "God isn't pleased with your decision, but I understand. If you pray hard enough and long enough, stay committed to your ministry and pay your tithes, God will eventually forgive you." But, no! They told me, "Congratulations!"

The most troubling part is that Heaven and Hell are generally the proverbial carrot and stick my faith tradition uses to keep us in check. Rule-keeping is tied to eternal life. If you follow the rules, you get to spend eternity with Jesus in heaven where the streets are paved with gold and we just get to worship all day (Sidebar: I love church, but non-stop worship is not my idea of heaven. Can we at least get a snack break?) On the other hand, if you don't follow the rules, you will spend eternity in hell where there is an all-consuming fire that burns forever. You will literally be set on fire and burn for an amount of time that your mind cannot fathom. And just for good measure, there will also be gnashing of teeth, which sounds incredibly uncomfortable to say the least. That is a lot of pressure. And what makes it even worse is that different faith traditions have different rules! And all Christian faith traditions claim that their rules are based on the Bible.

The reality is that Christians often confuse our doctrine with the Bible. We say, "we believe the Bible." But if we drill down, that statement should really be interpreted as "we believe our doctrine." Different faith traditions and denominations are generally separated by their doctrines, all of which they derive from the Bible.

For the sake of this discussion, I will define "doctrine" as a body of principles within a system of belief. As I mentioned above, sometimes the doctrines held by Baptist churches are different from the doctrines held by Pentecostal churches. But both churches are using the same Bible to formulate their doctrines.

The Pentecostal church may suggest that a Christian should not drink alcohol, citing scriptures like Proverbs 20:1, which says, "Wine is a mocker and beer a brawler; whoever is led astray by them is not wise." Or they may cite Ephesians 5:18 which says, "Do not get drunk on wine, which leads to debauchery. Instead be filled with the Spirit." Neither of these scriptures casts a positive light on alcohol. It seems safe to say that the Bible does not condone the use of alcohol. People who subscribe to this way of life rationalize it with their belief that they are following the Bible.

Then you have other faith traditions who are open to the use of alcohol based on their emphasis of other scriptures. An Episcopal church may highlight the story of Jesus' first public miracle, where he turned water into wine at a wedding celebration. It's important to note that the wedding party had already consumed the original supply of wine. So the attendees may very well have already been a little tipsy. These traditions may also cite 1 Timothy 5:23, which reads, "Stop drinking only water, and use a little wine because of your stomach and your frequent illness." Or they may cite Ecclesiastes 9:7, which states, "Go, eat your food with gladness, and drink your wine with a joyful heart, for God has already approved what you do."

We see two groups with opposing views on the exact same topic -- and both use the Bible to justify their stance! This is the danger in confusing the Bible with doctrine. Doctrines are created by emphasizing various scriptures that support a precept, while, at the same time, neglecting or reinterpreting the scriptures that contradict said precept. You can hold a biblical stance that we should avoid alcohol based on Proverbs 20:1. You can also hold a biblical stance that we embrace alcohol based on 1 Timothy 5:23. This is why I have a hard time reasoning with people who make declarations like, "I just believe the Bible!" Generally, my response is "What part?"

Christians believe our doctrines. And hear me clearly when I say this; doctrines are not inherently evil or divisive. I am not suggesting that we discontinue formulating doctrines. I believe that doctrines are necessary given the diversity of perspectives found in the Bible on various topics. Doctrines help to frame our system of belief. My critique here is that we should not confuse our doctrine with the totality of the Bible. Our doctrines are created by emphasizing certain portions of the Bible. When we confuse our doctrines with the totality of the Bible, we force ourselves to inaccurately reinterpret the parts of scripture that contradict our doctrine. And we ultimately rationalize the self-proclaimed supremacy of our doctrinal framework.

Biblical Contradictions

We will never be able to accurately identify the distinction between our doctrine and the Bible if we don't first acknowledge the contradictions in the Bible (This is the point where I generally lose people. I applaud you if you choose to keep reading.) Yes, I said it. THE BIBLE CONTAINS CONTRADICTIONS. Denying this truth is what makes our Rule-Keeping Theology fragile. Black church folk constantly chastise others for "picking and choosing" what we will follow in the Bible. What if I told you that oftentimes the Bible leaves us no choice?

Let's unpack one blatant example of a biblical contradiction that makes Rule-Keeping Theology unsustainable. If you have your Bibles, turn with me to the book of Proverbs, the 26th chapter, starting at the 4th verse. Let us all read together the 4th & 5th verses:

> 4. Do not answer fools according to their
> folly, or you will be a fool yourself. 5.
> Answer fools according to their folly, or
> they will be wise in their own eyes.

In the words of my dad, "Am I still in your Bible?" So should we follow verse 4 or verse 5? We can't possibly do both at the same time. So which one will you pick? Which one will you choose?

I had this conversation with a couple of friends who couldn't embrace the idea of biblical contradictions. One of them chose verse 4. The other friend responded, "It depends on the fool." Both of my friends and I come from religious backgrounds where we would be chastised for "picking and choosing" what to follow from the Bible. But that's what both of my friends did when they were confronted with these contradicting Proverbs. The uncomfortable reality is that the Bible leaves us no choice. The Bible is not a rule book for life. It is an invitation to use wisdom to determine what is prudent and just.

For almost every "biblical" concept there is another contradictory "biblical" concept. The question isn't whether we pick and choose. The question is how do we determine what to pick and choose? Yes, if your entire rule-keeping theological framework is built upon the consistency and inerrancy of scripture, Proverbs 26:4-5 is rather unsettling. I promise I'm coming around the corner with a warm blanket of embrace. But first we need to continue exploring the problem. "Problem with the Bible? What in the world do you mean when you say, 'Problem with the Bible,' Kristian?" I'm so glad you asked. You ask the best questions.

The Problem with the Bible

My theological evolution has been a lonely journey. I don't say that to diminish the valuable relationships that I have. I wouldn't trade them for the world. I'm grateful for people like Kervance Ross, Stephen Thurston, Jr., and Timothy Careathers who walked with me through my evolution and never stopped supporting and encouraging me. The loss of my larger community, however, was difficult. I stopped receiving invitations for speaking engagements. A few churches across the country who included me on an annual rotation rescinded their invitations. I was told by the pastor of a church I attended that there was no place for me in leadership at the church because of my views of biblical authority. I often tell Dave Garber that people like him and Chanequa Walker-Barnes (another one of my brilliant professors) educated me out of a job. You take a risk in the Black Church when you openly suggest the Bible contains flaws and contradictions. To my non-black readers, I'm sure you have similar experiences. I'm just speaking from my frame of reference.

Nonetheless, I pressed forward in my journey because once you learn something you can't unknow it. I kept writing and speaking my convictions as if my life depended on it. I knew there were other people that agreed with my train of thought. But I had not yet encountered anyone who openly and clearly articulated my train of thought. And then one fateful day, my friend Grayson Hester gave me a book and said, "You should read this. You and this guy sound a lot alike." The book he gave me is called *The Bible Tells Me So*, and the author is Pete Enns. I read that book and felt like I found my theological doppelganger. If you have never read any of his work, I encourage you to start today (finish my book first, of course).

What I am challenging us to do in this book and what I believe Enns challenges his readers to do in his many books is to shift our biblical paradigm. By paradigm I mean the framework containing basic assumptions, ways of thinking and methodology that are shared by members of a group. This book challenges us to shift the framework of basic assumptions Christians have about the Bible, our paradigm. Here's my feeble attempt to illustrate paradigm.

I have a god-sister named Quieter who is family to me. She has been a part of my life since birth. She helped raise me and has talked me through some of the most challenging times of my life. This example of how she shifted my paradigm is much more trivial though. One day when I was 8 or 9 years old, she took me to Scandia Family Fun Center in Fairfield, CA. After I was worn out on go-karts and arcade games we went to Denny's for dinner. Quieter ordered a burger and french fries with a side of ranch dressing. I was confused. In my limited life experience I had developed a basic assumption that ranch dressing was meant to be used for salads and nothing else. Quieter didn't order a salad, so why did she ask for a side of ranch dressing? What was she possibly going to do with this ranch dressing? It doesn't go on anything on her plate. I ordered my burger and fries with a side of ketchup because ketchup and only ketchup goes on french fries. This was my dipping sauce paradigm. I watched Quieter closely as she prepared to eat her ranch dressing. She said, "Little brother, have you ever put ranch dressing on your french fries?" I said, "Uggggggh! That's nasty." And in true Quieter fashion she replied, "Don't knock it until you try it, Little Brother." Because I trust Quieter (and I'm a foodie) I tried the ranch on my fries. And it CHANGED MY LIFE! Prior to that day I maintained a basic set of assumptions that ketchup goes on french fries and ranch goes on salad. Once Quieter flipped my paradigm on its head, I started dipping anything I could find in ranch dressing.

Christians need to have a Ranch Dressing Revelation in our relationship with the Bible. We come to the Bible with a basic framework of assumptions that hinders us from seeing all the ways it is meant to be used. Many of us have developed a biblical paradigm that views the Bible as an owner's manual, complete with step-by-step instructions on how to operate in life. And we believe if we follow each step according to the manual, we will spend eternity in heaven.

Pete Enns puts it this way, "The problem isn't the Bible. The problem is coming to the Bible with expectations it's not set up to bear." I didn't expect enough from ranch dressing. We Christians expect the wrong things from the Bible. We make claims of the Bible that it never makes of itself. I can't blame us. We are handicapped before we ever actually read the Bible.

Our Christian conditioning creates a paradigm that makes it difficult to read the Bible for what it actually says. Think about how kids are raised in church. We are taught plenty of Bible stories before we learn to read. We learn about Adam and Eve, Noah and the Ark, Moses parting the Red Sea, Daniel in the Lion's Den, Shadrach, Meshach and A Bad Negro, David & Goliath, the big fish that swallowed Jonah and many other stories. The key here is that we learn these stories before we can read. We are also generally conditioned to believe that whatever the Bible says is 100% historically accurate and serves as God's instruction for our lives. By the time we develop the ability to read, our biblical paradigm has already been established. The first time we encounter the Bible for ourselves we begin the experience with the following mindset, "This is the Word of God. It is always true and consistent. It contains no errors. I cannot question it or critique it. I must align and adjust myself to whatever I read in the Bible." This paradigm makes it almost impossible to read the Bible for what it actually says. Instead, we read into the Bible what we were conditioned to believe it says.

I once read an article about a presidential adviser in the Middle East who claimed he spoke on behalf of the Lord. He told the president of his country that God said the president needed to lead an attack on a neighboring country. He said God wanted him to do it because many generations ago, "the ancestors of the neighboring country were unfriendly to our ancestors." He advised the president that

God told him that they should kill every single person and animal in that country, from the oldest senior citizen down to the youngest infant. Well, guess what the president did? He attacked the country and killed everybody. The only advice he didn't take was to kill all the animals. The president planned on using the animals for some kind of ritual. The adviser told him that God was not pleased with him because he disobeyed a direct command. He told the president, "obedience is better than sacrifice."

The presidential adviser in this story is the Prophet Samuel. The president is Saul, the first king of Israel. The neighboring country is Amalek. This Bible story is told in 1 Samuel 15. Yes, we have quoted "obedience is better than sacrifice" out of context for generations. Samuel was basically saying, "Great job on obeying the order to kill everyone including the elderly and the infants. But I told you to kill the animals too." Keep in mind that the Amalekites were not actively attacking the Israelites. Nor is there any evidence in the story that the Amalekites were planning an attack. The Amalekites were not currently oppressing Israel. According to Samuel, God said to wipe them off the face of the earth based on some feud their ancestors waged with our ancestors.

We are taught in our schools, in our homes, and in our churches that genocide is evil and should never be excused. On the other hand, we are also taught in church that every command of God in scripture is righteous and must be obeyed. But what about when the biblical command of the Lord is to commit genocide? Those two lessons collide when we encounter the story in 1 Samuel 15. But our biblical paradigm causes us to read into the text what we want it to say rather than reading what it actually says. If we start with a set of basic assumptions that requires the Bible to be always right, we have to make sense of God saying commit genocide against an entire nation of people. As ancestors of people who survived the genocide of the transatlantic slave trade, this should make black people very uncomfortable because it sounds all too familiar.

Here's a question for your consideration: Do you identify with a God who calls for the genocide of men, women, children, and infants?

If your answer is "yes," you and I hold drastically different perspectives of God.

If your answer is "no," 1 Samuel 15 should concern you deeply, and you should consider the context the next time you say, "Obedience is better than sacrifice."

Don't worry though. I'm not suggesting that God is a genocidal maniac. A literal reading of scripture will definitely lead you to that conclusion. But I take the Bible way too seriously to always read it literally. The Bible is sacred, not sovereign. It is so important that we wrestle with this concept because it helps us understand how Greatest Commandment Theology works.

I converse with people almost every day about my theological lens. I'm having a hard time focusing on writing this book right now because multiple people are messaging me and asking for my thoughts on controversial issues. Usually people want to address a specific topic like alcohol or sexuality or cigars. We can't start the conversation by discussing the specific topic until we have established the paradigm from which we operate. I don't operate from the paradigm that suggests the Bible is always right and we must follow it word-for-word. If we have a conversation about a topic and you quote a scripture to me that bears no weight on my view of God, you'll be confused and frustrated because you assume, as a Christian, I view the Bible the same way you do. "Ok, Kristian, well, how do you view the

Bible?" I am so glad you asked. You really do ask the best questions.

Chapter 3

The Great Facebook Debate

It was a dark and gloomy night in November 2015. I was doing my normal browsing of Facebook posts, when I noticed one of my Facebook friends shared an article from BET.com entitled "Kirk Franklin Apologizes for Homophobia in the Black Church." The person who shared the article wrote the following caption: "I'll share my thoughts below, but I need some feedback. Thoughts?"

This began a series of comments from many members of the Black Church who disagreed vehemently with Kirk Franklin's statements. One person commented, "So should the church also apologize for bring(ing) about conviction for heterosexuals who commit fornication, or adultery? Now the church should watch it's condemnation of 'certain' sins. WHAT DOES THE WORD SAY CONCERNING ALL SIN…. I'm going to stop there (be)cause I feel my PRESHA going up!" This statement represents just one of dozens of comments people shared on this post and many other posts like it.

One commenter had the *unmitigated gall* (insert sarcasm) to suggest "being gay does not send you to hell." This comment received responses like, "Who said that?" and "I need you to explain, especially since you are a minister." One response said, "SIN sends you to hell… is that not a sin?" The anger and hostility that leapt from the typing fingers of these Christians troubled me. Worse still, they used Bible verses to justify their indignation.

I decided to engage the commenters in a dialogue about some of their statements concerning "THE WORD," as they put it. The majority of the people on the post were not interested in having a conversation about the issues that have plagued LGBTQ+ (Q+) persons in the Black Church for decades. They were more interested in using the Bible as a sacred canopy for their discomfort and hatred for same-gender attraction.

I entered the conversation to ask people to "consider the humanity of the situation without quoting scriptures." In the words of my professor, Dr. David Gushee, "Responsible Christian ethics requires moral reasoning and not just slapping a Bible quote on the issue." With that in mind, I encouraged the people commenting on the post to consider the enduring permanence of their own sexual orientations as they consider the plight of the gay Christian in the Black Church. My comments were met with a great deal of dissonance and disgust. In the subsequent responses, people compared same-gender-loving humans to pedophiles, murderers, and thieves.

These statements were quite unsettling for me, but I continued to press on with the conversation because I felt compelled to be a voice of reason. Of all the people who commented on the post, only one other person was interested in discussing the reasoning behind the issue, let alone the personal experiences of Q+ humans.

As the dialogue continued, I told the person who originally posted the article that we could talk about the issue in more detail in another venue. I advised him that we probably would not see eye-to-eye on every facet of the issue, but I am comfortable that we can "agree to disagree without becoming enemies." Immediately, another person (to whom I wasn't even speaking) responded to my comment with this question, "How do you agree to disagree if we believe in the same Word from the same God?" This question is representative of the biblical paradigm I unpacked earlier in this book, which suggests all the words of the Bible exist in harmony pointing to the perfect will of God. These views are dismissive of the fact that many people view the same texts in different ways and no person or group has a monopoly on the truth.

I continued the discussion, however, on the Facebook feed until a colleague of mine reached out to me in a private direct message. He served as a youth pastor of a megachurch which boasts a membership of approximately 22,000 people. He was following the comments on the aforementioned post. His initial message to me and the gentleman who shared the article said, "I'm interested in your view bro, just thought this would be a safe environment." The gentleman who shared the article then added a female acquaintance to the private message feed to make a total of four people, including me.

I encouraged all of them to consider again the personal experiences of gay people, especially gay Christians who are trying their best to live for God in light of what the Bible seemingly says about their sexual orientation. The conversation did not stay on topic for long because all three of them were more interested in hearing my take on what the Bible says about it.

I cannot discuss what the Bible says about sexuality without first establishing the paradigms from which we view the scriptures. I have come to the realization that when discussing any moral issue from a biblical perspective, the paradigmatic views of all parties involved must be taken into consideration. All of the individuals in the Facebook message approached the biblical conversation from a paradigm marked by biblical inerrancy and infallibility. As a result, they always approach the scriptures, regardless of the content, with the intent to reconcile and justify what they are reading.

My paradigm is drastically different. I approach the Bible with a historical-critical view that allows me to ask questions of and at times disagree with what I read. I told the people in the private message that I still believe the Bible contains the word of God. I do not, however, believe that God stopped speaking when men closed the canon in the 4th century. The church councils of the 4th century closed the discussion for what the Bible would contain. They did not close God's mouth.

I asked my discussion partners if they agree with everything in the Bible. They all answered "yes." As a follow-up question, I asked them, "Does it ever bother you that there is no biblical condemnation of Lot in Genesis 19 when he offers his two virgin daughters to a mob to be raped in order to protect his houseguests?" Below are the responses I received:

"Yes it does… But I don't think the story is told to show Lot's perfection, I think it shows his willingness to risk all to protect what he deems as holy…"

"I wondered about that, but I don't charge that to the Word. I charge that to Lot."

"Nothing happened to [Lot's] girls, which I believe was the rebuke of Lot's statement."

"Remember the time this took place in also. Women were property. No one was holding anyone accountable for doing right by them unless it was someone's wife. And the title of wife even was still property."

"Raping isn't right, but at least men sleeping with women wasn't an abomination."

I am almost ashamed to say this, but the last comment was made by the woman in the conversation, who happens to be a mother of daughters. All of these responses reflect a paradigm that suggests the Bible is the only word of God, and that it must be defended, rationalized, and justified at all costs. In this paradigm, even if what the individual reads runs completely contrary to reason, experience and their moral compass, because it is in the Bible, there must be a valid explanation -- even if it means saying a father offering his virgin daughters to be raped to death is preferred over same-gender sexual interaction.

I took the conversation a step further and challenged them to read the parallel story of the Levite's concubine in Judges 19. In this story, the life of the woman was not spared, and she was raped to death. None of them had ever even heard of this story, let alone read or studied it. But their paradigm required them to rationalize it. To my dismay, all of the individuals in this private message thread found illogical ways to justify the actions in this story, as well. As my friend Adam Gray said, "You can't rationalize the story of the Levite's concubine without sounding like an asshole."

The issue is that many Christians ascribe inerrancy to a Bible that they have not read and do not understand. The church has fostered Bible loyalty without Bible literacy. And as a wise person once said, the only thing more dangerous than ignorance is ignorance with enthusiasm. The Biblical indoctrination of many Christians runs so deep that we will reach for even the most obscure arguments to maintain the perceived credibility of our paradigm. Many of us are so tied to this idea of biblical inerrancy that we believe if the divine morality or factual historicity of the Bible ever comes into question, the entire Christian faith will be jeopardized.

What many Christians fail to realize is that this paradigm does not line up with our Western Christian practice. We actively practice a faith that does not follow every biblical directive verbatim. We practice a faith where Jesus clearly reinterprets long-held scriptural views established before his birth. We practice a faith where we behaviorally contradict biblical norms almost every day. We practice a faith whose sacred scriptures contradict themselves in certain places. There is discord between our paradigmatic beliefs and our daily practices.

Let me pause again to reiterate that I realize how uncomfortable this is. My theological evolution has been extremely uncomfortable. It's like learning your faith all over again for the first time. I experienced it myself and I have walked others through this process. If you can confront the discomfort and keep moving forward, I promise that freedom is on the other side. But freedom comes with a cost. It will cost you some comfort. It will cost you some normalcy. The worst part is that it will cost you some relationships. But what you experience on the other side of this wall is worth what you lose in the process.

Now back to where I left off. Pete Enns says that many of us have trouble understanding scripture because our paradigm requires "a Bible that behaves." We approach the Bible with a pre-established ideology and expect the Bible to substantiate it. And when the Bible doesn't behave the way we want it to, it results in cognitive dissonance; a state of mental discomfort resulting from one's conflicting attitudes, beliefs, or behaviors. That's what the people in the Great Facebook Debate experienced. One belief is that the Bible is always right. The second belief is that rape is always wrong. Then they were confronted with unfettered rape in the Bible and did not know how to process it: Cognitive Dissonance.

When I walk people through the process of learning how to engage the Bible without requiring it to behave a certain way, I lean heavily on a Prescriptive/Descriptive approach to scripture. Whether we admit it or not, as Christians, we all operate from a prescriptive/descriptive approach to the Bible. A prescriptive reading of scripture internalizes the content as being written directly to us. Prescriptive passages prescribe a way for us to relate to God, each other, and nature. For example, we read The Ten Commandments as prescriptive words written for us to follow.

Descriptive passages, on the other hand, are written to describe the way the writer and the writer's culture may have related to God, each other, and nature. Descriptive passages are written for us, not to us. There is much we can learn from descriptive passages, but they aren't to be followed like instructions in an owner's manual. For example, when many Christians are confronted with the various dietary laws in Leviticus (no shellfish, no pork), we don't read them as prescriptions for our lives. We read them as descriptions of the Ancient Hebrew culture. If you don't believe me, tell me the last time you went to a breakfast at your church that didn't include bacon or sausage. Tell me why church folk rush to Red Lobster for Endless Shrimp as soon as worship is over. These things are commonplace only as a result of a descriptive reading of certain scriptures.

I pause here to remind you that I am not arguing we need to start using a prescriptive/descriptive approach. I am suggesting that we already use this approach without realizing it. Be honest, you have read or heard something from the Bible before and thought to yourself, "That doesn't apply to today" or "That was written to a specific group of people." Don't worry. You didn't commit a sin by acknowledging that. God is not going to strike you down. God is comfortable with your questions and your doubts. The challenge is for *you* to get comfortable with them. Hopefully as you progress through these pages, your level of comfort will increase. If it doesn't increase, just read the book again and see if it works the second time.

I hear your thoughts. "Ok, Kristian. You have spent all of this time tearing down the Bible. So if the Bible contains errors and contradictions, what is the objective truth by which we should live our lives?" Thank you for asking. I swear you ask the best questions.

Chapter 4

We Need Structure!

Concretization

One of my favorite pastimes is smoking cigars. I enjoy it so much that I partnered with a few friends to create a whole ministry called Holy Smokes: Cigars & Spirituality. We started exclusively as a monthly gathering for people to come together and discuss life, faith and theology at Highland Cigar Lounge in Atlanta, GA where I live. The monthly gathering was so impactful that we decided to create the Holy Smokes: Cigars & Spirituality podcast using the monthly gathering as a template. On the podcast we use a Dollar Jar to monitor our cast members' language. In more conventional spaces the language being monitored would most likely be the use of profanity. Not at Holy Smokes. Profanity is allowed. We use the Dollar Jar to monitor academic words. A handful of geniuses who do this podcast with me tend to use words the regular people like me need to research on dictionary.com.

My friend and Holy Smokes cast member, Myron Randall is helping me edit this book and he keeps using words like "prolegomena" and "verisimilitude." I kid you not, I had to google these two words to figure out how to spell them. You should see how badly I butchered the spelling. Thank God Google knew what I was trying to say. I searched for "prolagamala." Google responded with "did you mean 'prolegomena?'" Yes, Google. That is exactly what I meant. Thank you, because I don't want to appear uneducated in my own book.

As you can see, we need a mechanism on Holy Smokes to keep these genius big-word-users in check. So when Myron or one of the other cast members uses a word like verisimilitude on the show without defining it for the audience, they have to put a dollar in the jar. Yes, I said "they" because it does not include me. They might argue otherwise, but this is my book, so there's that (Don't worry, I love my Holy Smokes family.) Every now and then I try to appear as smart as they are by throwing in a vocabulary word and defining it. In one episode I used the word "concretize" to explain my critique of the many expressions of progressive theology that I see. By progressive theology, I mean Christian-based movements that are shifting away from the rule-keeping biblical inerrancy paradigm I have been unpacking in this book. Let me be clear, in that episode I defined "concretize" before I used the word in a sentence, but everybody pounced on me to put a dollar in the jar like I just said "prolegomena" or something (I think my cast is turning on me.) Here is what I meant by "concretize": to give specific or definite form and structure to an idea. My critique of progressive theological expressions is that we have in large part not done an adequate job of giving specific or definite form and structure to our theologies.

We are trying to convince people that there is a better way to navigate our faith journey than simply avoiding activities on various biblical vice lists. We are trying to convince people that you can be in a good relationship with God without buying into the notion that, "the Bible says it. I believe it. That settles it." We are trying to convince people that we can walk in the way of Jesus Christ without subscribing to every directive of the Apostle Paul. The problem is when people ask for a concrete alternative to the rule-keeping theology they have always practiced, we respond with statements like, "you just gotta love people, man. Be kind and do justice." We sound like a bunch of hippies from the 1960's telling people to just get high on love and don't worry about anything else. That is not going to work. We need structure. We need form. We need our theology to be concrete.

I attended a conference a few years prior to the writing of this book that gathered a number of black progressive and conservative thought leaders, scholars and theologians to discuss controversial theological topics. It was a breath of fresh air because having started my theological journey with the rule-keeping paradigm, most of the conferences I was familiar with exclusively perpetuate rule-keeping ideology. I started thinking on a different wave and all of the sudden didn't know where to go. I didn't know what conferences were geared towards people who think like me.

There was a panel discussion at this theological conference where two progressive thinkers debated two conservative thinkers. I was so enriched by the clarity, insight and dexterity with which all of the panelists spoke on the topic of how to discern Truth. It is an interesting topic because of its abstractness. "Truth" is a funny word. Everyone has their own idea of Truth. All four of these thinkers were sharing their idea of Truth and what their truth is rooted in.

I remember one of the panelists leaning heavily into the Greatest Commandment where Jesus says love God and love your neighbor as yourself. Because the Greatest Commandment is the basis of this book, my heart leapt inside of my chest. His grasp of the importance of this concept within and beyond our Christian faith was so encouraging to me. But as I said above, I have been trained to state my case like an attorney since I was a little kid. I wanted this thinker to go further in concretizing what he meant because that's what his detractors on the stage and in the audience were waiting for. If you are going to flip my rule-keeping, Bible-believing paradigm on its head, you must give me something concrete on which I can stand.

Don't tell me that I don't have to put ketchup on my fries without letting me know that ranch is a viable substitute. I don't want dry french fries. I WANT A DIPPING SAUCE! Where is the dipping sauce?! Yes, fries can be eaten without a dipping sauce. But the sauce represents security. Rule-keeping theology offers the believer a level of security that abstract appeals to love do not offer. Abstract appeals to love are not invalid, but they lack the structure and form that most believers need in order to feel secure in their faith. This structure is particularly important when people's conditioning towards the rule-keeping paradigm began in their developmental years.

The Entrepreneur Fallacy

We live in a culture now where many young black people are starting businesses. Black women are the fastest growing group of business owners in the country. I am an entrepreneur two times over. I started a clothing business with my family in 2013 and I started a church in 2018. This trend leads a lot of pseudo-social media experts to suggest that, "Everyone should be an entrepreneur. Every person should be their own boss."

We unjustly shame people for working 9-5 jobs with a steady paycheck, pension plan, health benefits and sometimes their own office. I stand in the office of a prophet when I declare unto you the word of the Lord that entrepreneurship is not for everyone. It seems to be the sexy move in the 21st century among millennials. Hear me when I say this: IT IS NOT. Entrepreneurship is not sexy -- although it may appear that way on the surface.

People assume I'm winning in life because my clothes are so nice and I put them together so well. First of all, I didn't pay full price for my clothes. Second of all, my ability to style is a gift. And the Bible is correct when it says gifts come without repentance. In other words, we don't earn our gifts and we don't lose them either. Everyone is gifted in some way. Making money requires more than having a gift. My gift does not translate to me winning financially in life.

Entrepreneurship will take you through so many emotions in a given day. In the morning you feel like you are going to conquer the world. By lunch you feel like the biggest failure to ever start a business. By mid-afternoon you get a glimmer of hope because a client wrote you a good review. Right before you shut it down for the day, another client contacts you with a complaint, followed by news that one of your vendors is not going to keep their promise or take accountability for how to resolve it. Now you have to come out of your own pocket to fix the problem for your client. Then you go to a networking event to realize no one there fits your business profile and the drinks are overpriced, which sucks even more because you just spent money you didn't really have trying to fix the problem that you didn't create. And your client still may not do business with you again. And when you get done going through this rollercoaster of entrepreneurial emotions (all in the same day) there is no paycheck waiting for you on the 1st and the 15th. Entrepreneurship is one of the scariest things I have ever done. I left the security of consistent paychecks to sometimes withstanding two-month droughts in my income. Sure, the freedom is nice, but it costs me my security.

Telling a person indoctrinated in rule-keeping theology to abandon it based on abstract appeals to love is like telling a career nine-to-fiver to leave their paycheck, their pension, their cubicle and their health benefits to take a stab at starting a business from scratch with none of the security blankets mentioned above. The freedom looks appealing, but the risk doesn't seem to match the reward.

Fornicators!!!!!

It is a lot like the church's "no sex before marriage" ethic. The church says don't have intercourse or oral sex before you get married. Also, don't masturbate ever, married or not. If you do, God will be displeased with you and you could potentially go to hell. I hear your thoughts, "Well the Bible is clear on this issue and I agree with it." The Bible's clarity on sex outside of marriage is debatable, but let's work from that basic assumption for the sake of this discussion. Yes, the Bible is clear on this issue. The Bible is also set in a cultural context where kids were being placed in arranged marriages as early as 12 or 13 years old. That ethic applies much differently in our culture where we date before we get married to see if we even like the person, and the average age to get married in the United States is almost 30.

We tell kids all of the fabricated horrors of sex without ever telling them the pleasures. We lead them to believe something like, "If you have sex you will either get pregnant or contract a sexually transmitted disease for which there is no known cure and your life will be ruined and God will be ashamed of you."

Yes, this is highly problematic, but at least it provides some structure; Have sex = bad. Don't have sex = good. I can understand that. I don't like it. I think it sucks. But I can understand it. At least I will clearly know what God thinks about me based on how well I follow this rule. The biggest problem with this ethic though is that young people rush to get married before they are ready because their sexual desires are raging. We tell them during the courtship and the engagement that they have to wait until their wedding night to have sex. Women who have never explored their sexuality have bridal showers where they are gifted sexual items like lingerie and whatever other kinky toys their friends can fathom. Then after a lifetime of "no sex. No sex.

No sex" on that magical wedding night, voila!!!!! You can now have all the uninhibited sex your heart desires! Go ahead! Do all of the freaky stuff you have dreamed about! The bedroom is undefiled! It is a beautiful thing in the sight of God as he looks down upon you like a gleeful voyeur. Newsflash: this traumatizes many people. People have had to seek out religious trauma therapists -- like my wife -- to work through the damage of this overnight shift from "no sex because God hates it" to "all the sex because God loves it." I apologize if this illustration has triggered you because it chronicles your lived experience.

Inviting people to abandon the rule-keeping paradigm to dive head-first into "just love" can be just as traumatizing and unsettling. They wonder, "What will God think of me? What will my family and friends think of me? Am I going to go to hell?" Transitioning from the Rule-Keeping Paradigm to a Greatest Commandment Ethic should be done with great care and concern. If the new ethic does not provide any definite form or structure, it will be followed by as small a percentage of the population as there are full-time entrepreneurs. And many of its adherents will need therapy just to deal with the internal unspeakable horror they feel. Even with a measure of concretization, I have had people take years to painstakingly work through the fear of following this ancient framework for modern faith. "Ok, Kristian, so how do you make this concrete?" I am so glad you asked. You ask the best questions.

Chapter 5

Who Is My neighbor?

War of the Worlds.

The Book of Eli.

The Day After Tomorrow.

Independence Day.

World War Z.

These films represent just a small sample of the many films that highlight humanity's obsession with the end of the world. We are fascinated with the things that we cannot comprehend. This phenomenon is not unique to Hollywood. *New York Times* writer, Christian Lorentzen, put it this way, "We've been imagining the end of the world since we inherited it, and in most of our mythologies the world ceases to exist before it can begin." It seems like every time there is a natural disaster that strikes U.S. soil, inevitably someone is going to predict that this is a sign of the last and evil days. We tend to consider what is happening in our immediate vicinity to be a sign of God's intentions for all of humanity. I am especially tickled when American preachers predict the end of the world when a minor earthquake hits California but say nothing when a tsunami destroys an entire southeast Asian region.

In every generation we have seen and heard people predict the end times as a present reality. Paul warned in 1 Corinthians 7 that there was no pressing need to change your marital status because the end of the world was eminent. In every generation since Paul, Christians have been prophesying and prophe'lying that the end is upon us. When the truth is, Jesus said that no person knows the day nor the hour. It could be as soon as tomorrow. It may not be for another million years.

But whenever it is, we want to know what happens to us when this life ends. "Where will I go when I leave this world? If the heaven and hell I do or do not believe in exists, how do I ensure that I get to go to my preferred destination?" I apologize if that previous sentence made you uncomfortable. Well, actually, I'm not sorry. We need to be uncomfortable sometimes. Too often we assume that everyone in our spiritual network holds the same beliefs on every topic. I believe we need to make room for people to wrestle with what they believe without being chastised for their lack of belief. Not everyone believes in heaven and hell. By assuming everyone in our churches believes the same things, we silence those voices of dissent that could actually enliven our discussions and deepen our faith. Trust me, there are people in your church who aren't sure what they believe about heaven and hell. They probably just don't feel comfortable saying it because of how people would react. No group of people is monolithic, which means rigidly uniform in belief and perspective. If your church contains more than one person, it also contains a diversity of thoughts and beliefs. Embrace the discomfort and learn how to conduct a conversation centered on raising questions rather than dictating answers. The vast majority of us want to know what happens after we die, whether or not we are convinced of the existence of heaven and hell.

There is a pretty cool Bible story about a Samaritan that highlights this concern about the afterlife found in the 10th chapter of The Gospel of Luke. In the parable of The Samaritan an attorney asks Jesus "what must I do to inherit eternal life?" This is such an important question to address if people are going to seriously consider transitioning from rule-keeping to a Greatest Commandment framework. If we can't address this basic question we may as well just throw the whole theological framework away. The challenge in the story, however, is that the attorney didn't ask the question with the intent of learning something new. He arrogantly asked the question assuming he already had the answer. He was just trying to entrap Jesus, which was a constant theme in Jesus' brief ministry. Jesus was a witty and clever guy. He didn't just outright answer the attorney's question. He answered his question with a question because the attorney assumed, he already knew the answer. As I said before, sometimes we don't need answers for our questions. Instead we need questions for our answers.

Let me state at the onset that I am paraphrasing these quotes from the Bible story. If you desire to see the exact wording please follow along in Luke 10:25-37. My quotes will be heavily "Kristianized" as I walk through this story.

Now back to where I left off. To the question about inheriting eternal life, Jesus replies, "You're an attorney. You know the law. You tell me. What does the law say?" It's important to note that in Jesus' ancient Israelite culture there was no separation of church and state. The law of the land was synonymous with divine law. In other words, the attorney should *definitely* know the answer to this question.

The attorney's response is the basis for my entire ministry and the overall theme of this book. He replies, "You shall love the Lord your God with all of your heart, and with all your soul, and with all your strength and with all your mind; and your neighbor as yourself." It causes me great pain and anguish when I hear people talk about this commandment and minimize it to loving God and loving your neighbor. We cannot fully understand the magnitude of this commandment if we ignore the part about love for self. I will address this in more detail later.

Jesus replies, "Bingo! We have a winner! You didn't need to ask me that question in the first place. You were just trying to be slick. Now get out of my face." No, he didn't say all of that, but in my sanctified imagination I believe that's what he was thinking.

What Jesus actually said is, "Do this and you shall live," which is such a loaded response. The attorney asked about eternal life and Jesus responded with a statement about living in general. His response suggests that the formula for inheriting eternal life is the same formula for abundant living in this lifetime. I'm going to repeat that in case you read it too fast. According to Jesus' response, the formula for inheriting eternal life is the same formula for abundant living in this lifetime. Jesus never said, "I came that you might go to heaven." But he *did* say, "I came that you might have life and life more abundantly." In other words, if you put your energy in living abundantly in this life, according to the Greatest Commandment, the afterlife will take care of itself.

Let's continue with the story. The attorney was not satisfied with that reply. He needed Jesus to explain this theory further. He zooms in on the part of the Greatest Commandment which says, "love your neighbor as yourself" and asks Jesus, "Well, since you have all of the answers, then tell me who is my neighbor?" Let me translate what the attorney was asking. He wanted to know whom he could disqualify from the category of "neighbor" and expel to the margins. He wanted to know, "Who do I have permission to marginalize? Who are the people I can overlook? Who are the expendables that don't fit into this category? Surely, Jesus, you don't want me to love everybody as myself. That would just be preposterous. So, who can I leave off this list? Who is my neighbor?"

This question is so incredibly dangerous because we take so many inhumane actions when we attempt to marginalize people out of the "neighbor" category. The United States of America is a perfect example. Our country's wealth and dominance have been built and sustained by expelling an entire race of people to the margins of society. Black people haven't been considered "neighbor" because some people in power still aren't convinced that we are human. During slavery we were treated as property. During the Reconstruction era, we were viewed as lazy, incompetent savages. During the Jim Crow era we were treated as violent threats to the social order. And now in the age of mass incarceration and police brutality we are treated as super predators.

When a country disqualifies black people from the "neighbor" category it treats the crack epidemic that decimated black communities as a criminal crisis. When a country sees white people as neighbors, it treats the current opioid epidemic, predominantly sweeping through white communities, as a health crisis. The attorney is asking a dangerous question. And Jesus, like so many preachers, answered this question with a story.

He said, "A man was going down from Jerusalem to Jericho, and fell into the hands of robbers, who stripped him, beat him, and went away, leaving him half dead. Now by chance a priest was going down that road; and when he saw him, he passed by on the other side. So likewise a Levite, when he came to the place and saw him, passed by on the other side. But a Samaritan while traveling came near him; and when he saw him, he was moved with pity."

Here are a few notes to consider about this story. All of the characters with the exception of the Samaritan are people the attorney would naturally consider to be a neighbor. The Samaritan was the only outsider. To contextualize it, let's say the attorney was white (we know that he wasn't white. Jesus's life and culture was centered in the Northeast region of Africa. But indulge me for a moment.)

So Jesus says to this white attorney, "A 'white' man was going down from Jerusalem to Jericho and fell into the hands of 'white' robbers, who stripped him, beat him, and went away, leaving him half dead. Now by chance a 'white' priest was going down that road; and when he saw him, he passed by on the other side. So likewise a 'white' Levite, when he came to the place and saw him, passed by on the other side. But a 'black' Samaritan while traveling came near him; and when he saw him, he was moved with pity."

Ok. Maybe that didn't resonate with you. Let's try it again. Let's say the attorney was a Christian. (We know that he wasn't a Christian. Christianity didn't even exist yet. Jesus was a Jew and so was the attorney. But, indulge me for a moment).

Jesus says to the Christian attorney, "A 'Christian' man was going down from Jerusalem to Jericho and fell into the hands of 'Christian' robbers, who stripped him, beat him, and went away, leaving him half dead. Now by chance a 'Christian' priest was going down that road; and when he saw him, he passed by on the other side. So likewise a 'Christian' Levite, when he came to the place and saw him, passed by on the other side. But an 'Atheist' Samaritan while traveling came near him; and when he saw him, he was moved with pity."

The point of the story is that the Samaritan is supposed to be the character who is least likely to come to this man's rescue. First of all, it was the man's own people who robbed him and left him for dead. Second of all it was his own people who saw him half dead and crossed by on the other side of the road. Jesus uses two people who represent the community of faith to show how, in the words the words of Zora Neale Hurston, "Not all skinfolk are your kinfolk."

Jesus uses the priest, who represents the clergy, and the Levite, who represents the lay leadership/or support team of the church. Both of them are the first people the attorney would expect to help the man in need. (Not to mention the fact that it was his skinfolk who robbed him and beat him half to death in the first place!) Sometimes our rule-keeping theology emphasizes arbitrary spiritual rules over the well-being of people to the extent that we spiritually assault our own people. It reminds me of how some Christian doctrines have required women to remain married to their abusive husbands because of the doctrinal stance on divorce. We walk a dangerous line when we lift up our doctrines over people's lived experiences.

"Well, maybe the priest and the Levite had somewhere important to be. Maybe they just didn't have time." Don't let them off the hook. Jesus says they saw the man and intentionally passed by on the other side of the road. They didn't even care to inspect the situation on their way to their destination.

Scholarly theory suggests that the Levite did not approach the battered man on the side of the road because there was no way to be sure if he was dead or not. The ritual code of Jesus's cultural context said that if a Levite comes into contact with a dead body, they are declared ritually unclean and are unable to perform their role in the temple for a temporary period of time. So the Levite quite possibly overlooked this battered human's existence for the sake of not being kicked off the praise team. Obsessive rule-keeping causes us at times to be more concerned with saving souls than saving actual lives. Obsessive rule-keeping causes us at times to demean and diminish people in the name of deliverance. Obsessive rule-keeping causes us at times to practice homophobia in the name of holiness. Obsessive rule-keeping causes us at times to stifle people's gifts for the sake of the status-quo.

Jesus makes the most unlikely person in the story the hero. And Jesus never calls him "The Good Samaritan." Many people know this story as The Parable of The Good Samaritan. Many modern charitable organizations have been named after the "Good" Samaritan. I loathe this title. This is a quick lesson in how we read into the Bible what we want it to say. Nowhere in this parable does Jesus refer to the Samaritan as "The Good Samaritan." A translator or redactor came along and added that title to the story because the people in Jesus' culture held negative views of Samaritans, not unlike how many white people in America think black people are inferior. Adding "Good" to the title of the parable implies that this particular Samaritan is the exception. It suggests that Samaritans generally aren't "good" but this one stands out among the rest.

I liken it to white people referring to someone like me as the "articulate" black guy. It implies that black people generally aren't articulate. First of all, my proficiency in the King's English does not make me an exception among my people. If you don't believe me, watch any episode of *Holy Smokes: Cigars and Spirituality*. Second of all, speaking Ebonics does not mean one cannot articulate. It is oftentimes a matter of preference, not intelligence. Sometimes I prefer to use the slang of my culture to express myself. When I'm at the cookout, I may not feel like conjugating every verb and annunciating every syllable. My ability to articulate does not make me exceptional. And the Samaritan's acts of kindness do not make him exceptional. Maybe he typified what many

Samaritans were like, but the Israelites never took the time to get to genuinely know any of them. That was Jesus' whole point. To erroneously call this story The Parable of the Good Samaritan is to completely miss the message that Jesus was trying to convey. It's a story about prejudice. The people in the text had prejudice against all Samaritan people; whoever decided to name this story the "Good" Samaritan merely perpetuates that prejudice.

Let's continue with the remainder of Jesus' illustration to drive home the entire point:

> "But a Samaritan while traveling came near him; and when he saw him, he was moved with pity. He went to him and bandaged his wounds, having poured oil and wine on them. Then he put him on his own animal, brought him to an inn, and took care of him. The next day he took out two denarii, gave them to the innkeeper, and said, 'Take care of him; and when I come back, I will repay you whatever more you spend.' Which of these three, do you think, was a neighbor to the man who fell into the hands of the robbers?" He said, "The one who showed him mercy." Jesus said to him, "Go and do likewise."

There is so much in this text I could unpack. I'm sure if you are a preacher you have already conceptualized multiple sermon points to pull from this section. I am going to resist the urge to unpack this text line by line.

To summarize, the Samaritan chose to inspect the situation before concluding that the man was dead. Instead of crossing to the other side of the road he created intentional proximity, because that's what good neighbors do. The Samaritan spent his time and his money to help this battered man recover.

The major point I want to draw out of this story is the question that Jesus asks. "Which of these three, do you think, was a neighbor to the man who fell into the hands of the robbers?" Whenever I hear someone teach or preach from this passage, they usually emphasize Jesus' last statement: "Go and do likewise." I'm more intrigued by his question. We can teach that people of faith should show mercy in the same way that the Samaritan did in the text. The Samaritan is a wonderful example of a good neighbor. Don't stop teaching and subscribing to that ethic. But there is a deeper, more inconspicuous message in this story.

The attorney asked Jesus at the onset, "Who is my neighbor?" Jesus asks the attorney at the end of the parable, "Who was a neighbor to the man who got robbed?" Jesus wasn't telling this story to admonish people to be like the Samaritan. Again, let me reiterate that this is a viable message to get from this parable. But it wasn't the ultimate point. Jesus told the story in a way that challenges us to see ourselves as the man who was robbed and beaten. This man has no agency in this story. This man has no power.

If you want to identify who your neighbor is, don't ask yourself whose life you would save if they were in danger and you had the agency to do so. Ask yourself who would you allow to save your life if you were in danger and they had the agency. That's the question Greatest Commandment Theology asks us to consider. If Jesus calls us to love God in how we love our neighbor as a reflection of the love we have for ourselves, we need to know how to clearly define our neighbors.

Yes, your friends are always your neighbors, but your neighbors aren't always your friends. Your neighbor is the person you would allow to save your life if you were dying in a puddle of your own blood. It's easy to define your neighbor based on who you would save if they were in trouble. I once heard Dr. Ralph West say, "Confession is good for the soul and bad for your reputation." I'm going to risk my reputation with the following statement. There are some people I can think of right now who, if they were in danger, the most I would care to offer them would be thoughts and prayers. But identifying my neighbor shifts when I am the one in need.

So Jesus is saying, if your life was on the line and an Atheist person was the only help available to you, would you let them save your life? What if it were a Muslim or a Buddhist? or a redneck? or a racist? or a homeless person? or a felon? or a lesbian woman? or a gay man? or a bisexual person? or a trans person? If you wouldn't disqualify any of these people from saving your life, then they are defined as your neighbor, and the Greatest Commandment challenges you to love them based on the love you have for yourself. And if you would rather die than let one of these people save you, that says more about the lack of love you have for yourself than it says about what you think of them.

"Kristian, loving God and neighbor makes sense. I'm on the fence with emphasizing love for self. How do you make sense of this?" Thanks for asking. You never cease to amaze me with your brilliant questions.

Chapter 6

The Self-Love Stigma

I recently had a conversation with a black bible scholar for whom I have the utmost respect and admiration. She has a passion for justice, peace and honoring the full human dignity of every person created in the image of God. She understands the diversity of scripture and will be the first to tell you that the Bible indeed contradicts itself in certain places. She unapologetically teaches that the Bible was written by different people in different time periods in different cultures that had different perspectives of God. And these differences are represented in the Bible.

As I mentioned earlier, since I'm relatively new to this world of progressive theology, I relish opportunities to converse with other black theologians and scholars who share my views and can sharpen my perspective. She allowed me to share with her the Greatest Commandment Theological framework. I told her that I believe the Greatest Commandment is the basis on which we should build our theology. In the last section of this book I unpacked the Samaritan story where Jesus argues for the Greatest Commandment in the form of a story. But Jesus also shares this framework in a parallel passage in Matthew 22:36-40. In this passage Jesus adds some emphasis to it:

> "'Teacher, which commandment in the law is the greatest?' He said to him, 'You shall love the Lord your God with all your heart, and with all your soul, and with all your mind.' This is the greatest and first commandment. And a second is like it: You shall love your neighbor as yourself.' On these two commandments hang all the law and the prophets."

I shared with this scholar that I believe if Jesus says everything hangs on these two commandments, why not build our theology around it?

Since I was talking to a Hebrew Bible (Old Testament) scholar and I wanted to sound like I knew what I was talking about, I mentioned that Jesus is not presenting some new information. He was merely citing the Hebrew Bible. Jesus combined the commandment in Deuteronomy 6:4-5 with the commandment in Leviticus 19:18 to give us what we read in Matthew 22:36-40. I was secretly hoping I would get some brownie points for knowing that tidbit of Hebrew Bible information.

I shared with the scholar that I believe the problem with progressive theology is that we are working to fit a Greatest Commandment ethic into a Rule-Keeping framework. That's like trying to fit a square peg into a round hole. I suggested that instead of trying to force the Greatest Commandment to fit into our Rule-Keeping framework, we should start from scratch using the Greatest Commandment as the framework itself. We can then build around it. This conversation was going so well. I felt like I was really making an impression.

Then I shared my interpretation of The Greatest Commandment. That's where the conversation began to take a sharp turn. All of the brownie points I built up earlier in the conversation began to crumble before my very eyes. I told the scholar that according to what Jesus says in Matthew 22, our love for God is expressed in how we love our neighbor. And our love for our neighbor reflects the love we have for ourselves. So we can't fully love God if we don't love our neighbor. And we can't fully love our neighbor if we don't love ourselves. I told her that I believe love for self is at the core of the Gospel. She said, "Wait a minute. I disagree with that. That's a dangerous proposition.

Love for self leads to some problems." My head dropped. I just knew she would immediately see where I was coming from, but even a Bible scholar who practices her faith as an ongoing work of justice-seeking said that love for self was too much of a reach.

It was in that moment I realized that this may be one of the most difficult aspects of Greatest Commandment Theology to sell. I understand it to a degree. Many people pervert the notion of self-love as an excuse to do whatever they want, regardless of how it affects other people. Some people use self-love as a justification for arrogance and haughtiness. We all have that one person in our life or our social media feed who is disrespectful and dismissive of others, who then seals their self-absorbed rants with, "I don't care what ya'll think because I LOVE ME!" This is likely the picture that people have in mind when I suggest that love for self is at the core of the Gospel. I believe the stigma around self-love is one of the biggest challenges facing people of faith who want to learn to truly love one another. How can we love one another when we are uncomfortable loving ourselves?

Maybe our discomfort is rooted in our understanding of the scriptures. As we established earlier, those of us who believe in heaven and hell don't want to run the risk of going to hell. And from generation to generation we are constantly obsessing over the end times. And according to 2 Timothy 3, loving ourselves is not something we should aspire to achieve. Look at what the text clearly says in verses 1-5:

> You must understand this, that in the last days distressing times will come. For people will be **lovers of themselves**, lovers of money, boasters, arrogant, abusive, disobedient to their parents, ungrateful, unholy, inhuman, implacable, slanderers, profligates, brutes, haters of good, treacherous, reckless, swollen with conceit, lovers

> of pleasure rather than lovers of God, holding to the outward form of godliness but denying its power. Avoid them!

I'll be honest. I don't even know what some of these words mean. They sound like words that Kervance, Myron or Grayson would use on any given episode of *Holy Smokes: Cigars and Spirituality*. What I *can* gather from this text is that this list of attributes is not flattering. At the end of the passage, the reader is advised to avoid people with these attributes including those who are lovers of themselves. Could it be that I am trying to usher in the last days with this heretical book that emphasizes love for self as the core of the Gospel? You might be surprised when you look closer at what the text says.

Let's start by acknowledging that the Bible was not originally written in English. The Hebrew Bible, aka Old Testament, was originally written in Hebrew and the New Testament was originally written in Greek. Some Christians suggest that the Bible doesn't require interpretation because it is the Word of God and it says what it says. But the process of translation is an act of interpretation. You cannot translate a document without interpretation. Even the words of Jesus have been interpreted and reinterpreted over the years. Always keep in mind that when we read the words of Jesus, we are reading an English translation of a Greek text about a man who spoke Aramaic and quoted Hebrew scriptures. It is inevitable for some things to get lost in translation. If you are still holding to the biblical inerrancy paradigm, this probably makes you very uncomfortable. If you have evolved beyond that framework then hopefully my little play on words was impressive. If you are still having a hard time understanding how translation requires interpretation, let me try to contextualize it.

Let's imagine that someone is new to the English language and they are trying to translate a document written in the common language of the author. I say common language because there are many things, we take for granted in our everyday speech, that would thoroughly confuse a non-English speaking person. We all use idioms on an almost daily basis. (An idiom is a statement that consists of words whose definitions do not explain the meaning of the statement.) If you are saying to yourself, "Well, that definition just went over my head," you have just used an idiom. "Went over my head" means something totally different than the sum of the definitions of the words in the statement. "Went over my head" is an idiom for "I do not understand what was just said." Common language phrases like idioms get lost in translation. The New Testament was written in Koine Greek, which was the common language of that culture. This challenge in translation is not limited to phrases. It could be one solitary word that "throws a person off" (you see what I did there? Another idiom).

And the issue of translation isn't even unique to people who don't speak the original language. We can run into interpretation issues when everyone speaks the same language but has different cultural backgrounds. Take for instance the English word "dope." The academic definition of "dope" is "any thick liquid or pasty preparation, as a lubricant, used in preparing a surface."

The most popular definition in the Urban Dictionary for "dope" defines it as "1) the term for marijuana used by those who do not do drugs, 2) the term for heroin for those who only smoke marijuana or 3) a descriptive term used to denote how good or pleasing something is."

As a millennial member of the Hip Hop Generation, I did not know the academic definition of "dope" until I looked it up so I could include it in this book. My culture determined how I came to use the term. Another person unfamiliar with Hip Hop Culture who uses the term in a more academic sense would be perplexed if I used the term in its descriptive slang form by stating, "That car is dope." It is amazing that two people who speak the same language, living in the same city, state and country can interpret the same word in two totally unrelated ways, yet some people believe that the Bible, written thousands of years ago in a foreign culture, country, era and language, does not require interpretation.

With that in mind, we need to consider what gets lost in translation when we compare the language of the Greatest Commandment in Matthew 22 to what we read in 2 Timothy 3. We also must always consider the context of what we are reading. Never forget this: If you take a text out of its context, all you have left is a con. Don't be conned into believing the wrong thing because you have allowed someone else to extract a text from its context.

The English translations of Matthew 22 and 2 Timothy 3 use the term "love" and connect it to the self. There's just one problem. The English language does not place nearly as much emphasis on the concept of love as does the Ancient Koine Greek. The English language features one word for love. Regardless of the type of love we are explaining we say "love." Whether we are expressing love to our spouse, parent, friend, pet, favorite sports team, or favorite food, we say "love."

Ancient Greek contains at least 4 different root words for "love." Would you believe me if I told you that the Greek word for love in Matthew 22 is different from the Greek word for "love" in 2 Timothy 3? Well, you don't have to take my word for it. Feel free to fact check me. But I'm going to tell you the difference anyway. I promise not to turn this book into a lesson on Greek, but I need to at least make sense out of these two seemingly contradictory passages. It would be irresponsible of me to tell you that your love for God is rooted in your love for yourself and not address the fact that the Bible also says lovers of self should be avoided.

The root Greek word for "love" in the Greatest Commandment is "agape." It is a general love for all of God's people. It is the love tied to the basic human dignity of each of us created in the image of God. If we had a term for "agape" in English there wouldn't be that awkward situation when one person tells their love interest for the first time, "I love you," and the other person responds, "Wait a minute. Do you mean you love love me? Like... in love with me?" The Greatest Commandment calls us to love our neighbors and ourselves in a way that honors the image of God in each of us. I have to recognize the image of God in myself to recognize the image of God in my neighbor. We tend to overlook love for self in the Greatest Commandment because Jesus seems to assume that people love themselves. There is no directive to love yourself because it is assumed that you do. That is a dangerous assumption. Most humans don't even know what it means to genuinely and holistically love ourselves. We can't quote The Greatest Commandment under the assumption that everyone has already mastered love for self. We can't master something we're unwilling to even discuss.

The love to which the writer refers in II Timothy 3 is "philautos," which means a self-absorbed, selfish form of love. It means someone who is overly impressed with oneself. It does not honor the image of God in our neighbor. This type of love reflects a form of self-intoxication.

Unfortunately, when I share with people that we have to love ourselves in order to fully love our neighbors and ultimately love God, they picture a "philautos" form of love rather than an "agape" form of love. "Philautos" loses sight of the fact that we are all created in the image of God. "Agape" recognizes that I bear the image of God, but in the words of my friend Grayson Hester, "Thank goodness God doesn't look like me. Thank goodness the image I bear is not the whole image."

I believe this is where I lost the scholar in that conversation. We don't have the language to differentiate between the various forms of love represented in scripture. And when I suggest the importance of us loving ourselves, we tend to conflate it with being intoxicated with ourselves. The love for self that Jesus implies in the Greatest Commandment recognizes that at least in part, my neighbor is my connection to God. We should have a personal, private relationship with God. We should also recognize that our relationship with God is just as much horizontal -- from person to person -- as it is vertical -- from person to divinity.

Love for self recognizes the importance of meaningful relationships. If I don't nurture meaningful relationships, I am missing a major component of what it means to love myself. If I don't nurture meaningful relationships, maybe I actually should be avoided like the people to whom II Timothy 3 refers. Good news: I continued the conversation with the Bible scholar. She gave me my brownie points back after I explained what I meant by "self-love."

"But Kristian, how is love for my neighbor tied to love for myself?" Thank you for asking. Your questions are always on point! (Another idiom.)

Chapter 7

A Word from Tom Hanks

I used to think I liked movies and cinema until I met my wife, Pamela. It was at that moment I realized I am just a novice. She is a fanatic. An ideal day off for her is laying around watching movie after movie, whether or not she is familiar with the movie. She's one of the only people I know who will start a movie she has never encountered before, realize half-way through it is a terrible film and keep watching it because she is committed to seeing how it ends, no matter how terrible it is. And that is her idea of relaxation. I have come to grips with the reality that I am just a casual movie watcher.

Some of my favorite male actors include Denzel Washington (The GOAT), Jeffery Wright, Steve Carrell, Jamie Foxx, and Christian Bale. Although Denzel is my personal greatest of all time, Tom Hanks has a special place in my heart. Ever since I watched him in the film *Big*, I have been a huge fan. I quote a line from *Forrest Gump* almost every other week. One of Hanks' most impressive films, in my opinion, is *Cast Away*. I am convinced that anyone who can make an award-winning, blockbuster film featuring a volleyball as the primary supporting character deserves to be on an All Time Greats list. It doesn't hurt that Tom Hanks in *Cast Away* teaches one of the most valuable lessons we can ever learn. We as human beings are created for relationships.

Before we explore *Cast Away*, let me take a moment to address the science that undergirds the message we see in scripture and cinema. One of the most valuable lessons I learned in my required undergrad psychology course at Alabama A&M University was about the work of American psychologist Abraham Maslow. He created what is known today as Maslow's Hierarchy of Needs. It suggests humans have an array of needs that allow us to achieve our optimum level of survival, sanity, satisfaction, and success. The model is depicted as a pyramid with basic physiological needs as the foundation and self-fulfillment needs as the apex.

Maslow suggests that these needs are best addressed in order from the foundation to the apex of the pyramid. Physiological needs like food, water and air should be met before a person has the bandwidth to pursue their greater purpose in life.

I liken it to stories my wife would tell me about doing community-based mental and behavioral health work with school-aged kids. She had some clients who were struggling to meet their basic needs like having enough food in the fridge. She understood she needed to address their physical hunger before they would even attempt to address their behavioral challenges. One need comes before the other.

That is the basic premise of Maslow's Hierarchy. Level One (most important) includes needs such as food, water, air, warmth, and rest. Level Two includes needs for safety and security. Level Three includes meaningful relationships, both romantic and platonic. Level 4 and Level 5 consist of needs for prestige, esteem, accomplishment and achieving one's full potential. Notice the importance of relationships in Maslow's Hierarchy. Once a human has secured air, water, food, safety, and security (the basic needs for survival) the very next level of needs are relationships (basic needs for sanity). Humans are not wired to pursue satisfaction and success if we have not first addressed survival and sanity. *Cast Away* is the perfect depiction of this reality.

Spoiler Alert: I am going to give away the plot of the film. Tom Hanks plays a character named Chuck Noland who is a global systems analyst for FedEx. On a holiday business trip to Malaysia, taken to address a system problem, his FedEx plane hits a violent storm and crashes in the Pacific Ocean. As the lone survivor, Chuck floats on a life raft to a deserted island. Some packages from the plane also float to the deserted island, including one which contains a volleyball. After his traumatic experience, Chuck gathers himself and explores the island to discover that it is uninhabited. He concludes that he might be stuck here for a while.

He then figures out where he can find some food and water on the island (Level 1). Next, he finds shelter in a cave to protect himself from the elements (Level 2). At this point, Chuck has everything he needs to survive. He has learned how to feed himself and shelter himself from climatic extremes. This is the basis of human needs for physiological health. But one day he gashes his hand with a stick while struggling to make a fire and almost has a mental breakdown. In his rage and frustration, he picks up the volleyball with his bloody hand and hurls it with all his strength. Chuck is about to go crazy, not because he is hungry, not because he doesn't feel safe. He has already addressed those needs. He's about to snap not because he's penniless or because he lost his job. None of those things is even important to him right now. He's about to snap because he's lonely. He has no one with whom he can share his life experiences.

Later he picks up the blood-covered volleyball. He draws a face on the ball, names it Wilson, and commences to have a full-blown relationship with him. Wilson ultimately becomes Chuck's saving grace during the four years he spent on that uninhabited island. Chuck confided in Wilson, laughed with Wilson, cried with Wilson, fussed at Wilson, and depended on Wilson. Chuck maintained his sanity by relating to Wilson. His bond with Wilson was so strong that it became the one thing that gave him a reason to continue living.

When Chuck finally finds a way to get off the island on a makeshift raft he created, he takes Wilson with him. He has no idea what will happen when he gets out to sea, but as long as he has Wilson by his side, he has hope.

In one of the saddest scenes of the movie, Wilson gets separated from the raft and irretrievably drifts away. At that very moment, Chuck gives up on survival. He resolves to lie on his raft and die because the only relationship he had known for the past four years ended. Chuck's life lost meaning without the one meaningful relationship he had. A life without relationship is a life not worth living. If you don't believe this to be true, do some research about the torment of solitary confinement in the U.S. prison system. Separating people from all human contact is a form of torture.

Maybe examples from science and cinema are not strong enough evidence for you that relationships give meaning to life. How about some scripture? I would never suggest that we need to decentralize scripture as we reconsider rule-keeping theology in favor of Greatest Commandment Theology. We do, however, need to undeify scripture. In other words, we need not make the Bible out to be a God in and of itself. It contains some of the greatest wisdom the world has ever known, even though it itself is not God.

Let's take it all the way back to the creation story in Genesis. I'm not going to assume everyone reading this book knows the story, so let me give you the CliffsNotes. God created the world in six figurative days and rested on the seventh day. In one version of the story, God created male and female at the same time. In another version of the story, God created the male first.

Each time God created an aspect of our world, God saw that it was good. God created light and saw that it was good. God created land & sea and saw that it was good. God created trees and plants and saw that they were good. God created fish, wild animals and birds and saw that they were good. Our favorite part of the story is where God notices how good everything is. We rarely point out that not everything God did in creation was good.

The Bible specifically says that there was one aspect of creation that wasn't good. In Genesis 2, God noticed that the man -- whom we know as Adam -- was alone, and God said, "That's not good." God saw that Adam had no one with whom to share life. He had no meaningful relationships other than his relationship with God. In the words of my friend Nikki Hardeman, this suggests that, "sometimes God alone isn't enough." I know that may rattle your theological sensibilities, but I'm merely pointing out what the scripture implies. I know we like to say God is all we need and we "don't need nobody else," but, according to Genesis 2, that's not true.

If God is all we need, there would have been no need for God to find a companion for Adam. Let me not also fall into the trap of reducing this story to a glorification of romantic relationships as the only viable way to enjoy companionship. I'm not in the business of shaming single people for not finding someone to marry. This story is about relationships in general, not marriage. Once God recognized that Adam needed a companion because God alone wasn't enough, the Creator presented Adam with all of the animals to see if Adam could find a suitable companion. None of the animals were able to truly fill Adam's need for meaningful relationship. So God created a complementary companion in Eve. And at that point God could finally say, "Now, that's better."

Humans are created for relationship. Without meaningful relationships our lives have no meaning. Science, cinema, and scripture all support this idea. 1 John 4:20 reinforces this aspect of the Greatest Commandment by saying,

> "Those who say, 'I love God,' and hate their brothers or sisters, are liars; for those who do not love a brother or sister whom they have seen, cannot love God whom they have not seen. The commandment we have from him is this: those who love God must love their brothers and sisters also."

Our love for God can only be fully understood through how we love our neighbors as ourselves. I have found no other viable option to clearly articulate what love for God looks like. The Greatest Commandment functions much like Maslow's Hierarchy of Needs.

Love for God is the apex.

Love for neighbor is the connection.

Love for self is the foundation.

Yes, you read that right. Love for self is the foundation. I'll say it one more time for the people in the back: LOVE FOR SELF IS THE FOUNDATION.

It starts with God's undying love for us. Our lives should be lived as a response to how God first loved us. The way we express that love back to God is in how we love our neighbors as ourselves. We can't love God fully if we don't understand how to love ourselves. When I discuss this topic with people this is how it usually goes:

Them: "No, Kristian. You have to love God first. That is where it all starts."

Me: "Cool, so how do I love God?"

Them: "By following His will and His way."

Me: "Cool, what is His will and His way?"

Them: "God says that those who love me will keep my commandments."

Me: "Cool, which commandments? Are we to keep every commandment? What about the commandments we have written off as irrelevant or descriptive? Who decides which commandments still apply and which commandments don't apply? Your parents? Your pastor? Your bishop? Your priest? Your denomination? The Council of Nicea? Who?"

Them: "Well…"

Me: "I agree with you in part. Let's tie our love for God to keeping God's commandments. Since there are a diversity of commandments in scripture, some of which we subscribe to and others we don't, how about we start with the Greatest Commandment?"

Love for God is not a self-defining concept. It is abstract at best and paralyzingly daunting at worst. If we are going to tie our entire faith to loving God, we better have a way to make that applicable and tangible. We can't say you love God by loving God. We have to be able to put our finger on what loving God looks like.

Jesus said in Matthew 22 that everything hinges on love for God and love for neighbor as self. That implies that he did not give two separate commandments. He stated one Greatest Commandment with two parts. Jesus does not give us the wiggle room to separate love for God and love for neighbor as self. They are inextricably linked. Love for neighbor as self is love for God. Love for God is love for neighbor as self. I can't explain love for God without unpacking love for neighbor as self. I can however give you some tangible ways on how to love yourself. And then maybe that will resolve some of the ambiguity of how to love God. Like I said earlier, if we invite people to live a love ethic that lacks form and structure, we are setting them up for failure.

"Ok, Kristian, I hear you. I'm not sure if I agree, but I can somewhat understand your angle. Here's the gaping hole in your theory though: what about sin? Is there no such thing as sin anymore?" Oh, that is the best question you've asked yet! You really do ask the best questions.

Chapter 8

Well What About Sin?

I went to a conference hosted by the Cooperative Baptist Fellowship in 2019 where I attended a seminar led by a LGBTQ+ (Q+) brother focused on how to effectively minister to Q+ persons in our churches. This brother spoke from his heart about his love for God and his desire for Q+ persons to be able to freely serve God in their local churches without being treated like lepers. My one-sentence synopsis of the seminar is that churches should grant Q+ persons basic human dignity.

He told a story about a stray dog that used to walk through his neighborhood every day when he was a little kid. A group of boys who gathered daily outside of a house would throw rocks at the stray dog every time it walked by. And every time one of the rocks hit the stray dog, it would whimper in pain. This routine went on day after day, week after week, month after month. Until, one day the dog walked through the neighborhood, and the boys weren't gathered outside. Thankfully, on that day the dog wasn't hit with rocks. Ironically, however, when the dog walked past the house where the boys would normally be gathered, it whimpered in pain as if it were hit by the rock. The dog had become so accustomed to being hit by rocks; the very sight of the house triggered the pain he had felt every time he walked by before.

This Q+ brother said to us in that seminar, "That is what it is like for many LGBTQ+ people whenever we pass by a church." The church has thrown so many spiritually abusive rocks at Q+ people that they can't even walk past a church without wincing. That story hit me in the chest like a ton of bricks. As a representative of this stone-throwing, death-dealing church, I felt like trash.

This brother -- who appeared to be in his mid-40s -- also mentioned that one of the figurative rocks continuously hurled at him when he was young was the term "queer." Many people in the Q+ community have reclaimed this term that straight people used for evil in the past. They have repurposed it as a term of endearment and empowerment. But this brother said that the term had caused him too much personal damage to reclaim it.

I can relate to that sentiment because there are many people in the black community who refuse to use the word "nigga." The term has been too harmful to them in the past for them to feel it is worthy of being reclaimed in the present. Although I use the term frequently, I respect those who choose not to. I also would not accept someone outside of my community using that word in reference to me or any other black person. As such, I decided, based on this brother's testimony that I would refrain from using the term "queer."

In any effort to maintain my linguistic laziness, instead of saying LGBTQ+ every time I refer to that community, I have coined the term "Q+". The "Q" in "Q+" can mean questioning or queer because some people are comfortable with the term queer while others prefer to use "questioning" to refer to those who are still in the process of discovery. It's safe to say that this brother's story touched my heart.

His appeal was for the Church to see the same image of God in Q+ people that we claim to see in everyone else. Towards the end of his heartfelt presentation, he opened up the floor for questions. One of the audience members raised her hand. Once he acknowledged her, she dismissively asked,

"Well, is there any such thing as sin anymore?" That is the exact same question I am frequently asked when I talk about the framework of Greatest Commandment Theology.

Our obsession with identifying and defining sin is tied to our obsession with heaven and hell. We want to clearly know what actions are considered sins so that we can try our best to avoid them. We need rules to follow. The problem is that every religion, denomination, church, and household has a different set of sins.

No one can agree on what all is considered a sin because sins are a cultural phenomenon. The concept of sin is universal. Sins, on the other hand, are cultural. Everywhere you go in every culture there is a concept of right and wrong. But different cultures have varied perspectives on *what* is right and wrong. I mentioned earlier in the book that some traditions consider the consumption of alcohol a sin, while others do not. Some traditions consider billiards a sin, while others do not. Some traditions consider not observing Saturday as the Sabbath Day a sin, while others do not. Some traditions consider polygamy a sin, while the Bible does not. I could do this for days, but I think you get the picture. We claim to use the Bible to define what sin is, but we really don't. We have already discussed a number of actions we consider sin that the Bible does not and vice versa. If sin is such a paramount issue, shouldn't we have a better grasp on how to define it?

People assume that my theology dismisses the notion of sin. The reality is that Greatest Commandment Theology provides the clearest universal framework for sin that I have encountered in my brief time on this earth.

Let's start from the top. Jesus says that the Greatest Commandment is that we love God in how we love our neighbor which reflects the love we have for ourselves. He goes on to say that everything hinges on this commandment. Using this framework, we can define "sin" as anything that harms me or harms my neighbor. The question we must ask ourselves is, "If it doesn't harm me, and it doesn't harm my neighbor, why am I so convinced that it harms God?"

I know -- too easy, right? It can't possibly be that simple. You want me to give you a list of 613 commandments you must follow in order to be in the will of God. Sorry, that's not going to happen. Greatest Commandment Theology is not a rule book. It is a framework. It doesn't allow its adherents to outsource the responsibility of their life decisions onto another spiritual authority, like their pastor or their bishop or the Apostle Paul. Within this framework, you have to truly, in the words of the elder saints, "Work out your own soul's salvation."

I hear your thoughts. "That just seems way too simple." You're not sure if you want to stake your eternal life on something so simple when you have been trying, up to this point, to unsuccessfully practice such a complex rule-keeping theology up to this point. Nonetheless, Jesus stakes his theological claim here, so I will do the same.

If the Greatest Commandment is to love, then anything that contradicts love is a sin. The first rule of love is "do no harm." You can't help everyone. But you can at least try not to harm anyone, including yourself. At the same time, it's important not to get bogged down with the indirect, unintended, far-removed consequences of every action that you take in this globalized world. For more on this, travel with me to The Good Place.

The Good Place is a comedy television show loosely based on the premise of rule-keeping theology. It tells the story of four people who have passed on to the afterlife where they discover that deceased people are sent to "The Good Place" or "The Bad Place" based on a point system. Points are added when people do good things and points are subtracted when people do bad things. If you earn enough points during your life you get to go to The Good Place. If you don't get enough points you get sent to hell… I mean The Bad Place. It's a great show that I recommend you watch if you enjoy comedy or philosophy or ethics.

There is one scene where Michael, the demon played by Ted Danson, is trying to convince the Judge -- played by Maya Rudolph -- that the point system is broken. He said, "Your Honor, I once stood in front of you and said I thought there was something wrong with the point system. I finally know what it is. Life now is so complicated. It's impossible for anyone to be good enough for the Good Place… These days just buying a tomato at a grocery store means that you are unwittingly supporting toxic pesticides, exploiting labor, contributing to global warming. Humans think that they are making one choice. But they're actually making dozens of choices they don't even know they are making." Unfortunately, the Judge with her staunch commitment to the rule-keeping point system, completely dismissed Michael's assessment as trivial. I sure hope The Great Judge isn't as dismissive as the fictional judge in *The Good Place*. If so, we are in big trouble.

It isn't psychologically, emotionally, or spiritually healthy to obsess over every minute detail of every decision we make. We wouldn't be able to function. Think about it: do you know the entire process of creating the smartphone that you carry on you every day? Probably not. Chances are a laborer was exploited somewhere in the supply chain from raw materials to the phone landing in your hand. The Greatest Commandment is not calling you to disavow your smartphone and tablet in the name of love.

What I believe The Greatest Commandment calls us to do is avoid active affliction. Do not cause intentional harm to yourself or your neighbor in a way that disregards their humanity. Do not oppress. Do not demean. Do not belittle. Do not tear down. Do not disregard. Do not engage in active affliction of anyone, including yourself. As you avoid active affliction, do advocate for the oppressed. Do challenge the systems that cause harm to others. Do the work of justice.

Oftentimes when we see a person mistreating other people, it is *not* based on what that person thinks of other people. It is generally based on a deficiency they have within themselves. If a person is insecure, they project that insecurity onto others. If a person is full of self-hatred, they project it onto other people in hateful ways. Men who constantly demean women, generally operate from a place of fragile masculinity. People who are the most vocal in their disdain for Q+ persons often have an internal struggle with their own sexuality. They can't possibly love other people because they don't know how to love themselves.

The inverse is also true. People who are full of agape love for themselves, project that love onto others. Those who are full of compassion for themselves, will project compassion onto those around them. Those who extend grace to themselves as they evolve, will extend grace to others. Humans project externally what we possess internally.

Harm vs. Discomfort

As we consider the "do no harm" ethic woven into the command to love, it is important that we do not confuse "harm" with "discomfort." This is the biggest mistake people make in their attempts to understand The Greatest

Commandment framework. Harm and discomfort are not the same.

Harm is an act of imposing one's will onto another person in a way that hinders them from living their life in a meaningful and just way. I often see this when people in privileged groups diminish the cries for justice and equality by oppressed people.

Privilege is definitely one of the trigger words of our generation. It makes people uncomfortable because it feels like an attack. Privilege is not a sin. Privilege is not something that a person earns. It is granted to them. Inheriting privilege is not sinful, but it does come with responsibility.

I didn't earn the privileges that come with being a straight black male in the Black Baptist Church. I didn't earn the opportunity to have other people assume my voice is powerful and authoritative based on my gender and sexual orientation. It was bestowed upon me.

Some white people often say they do not have privilege because their whiteness did not afford them any advancements in life. Some argue that they grew up poor and had to struggle for everything they earned. I won't discredit white people's lived experiences. I will say, however, that privilege is not exclusively defined by what you are given. It is also defined by immunity. Even if a white person was never given anything because they are white, their whiteness has made them immune to race-based systemic discrimination.

I'm not talking about being offended because a black person called you "Karen." I am specifically talking about the systems of white supremacy that are woven into the fabric of America, systems that specifically oppress non-whites. If you want to explore this concept in further detail, read *I Bring the Voices of My People* by Dr. Chanequa Walker-Barnes and *The Color of Law* by Richard Rothstein.

The Greatest Commandment challenges all of us to first acknowledge our privilege and refuse to rest in it at the expense of others who do not share our privilege. Unacknowledged privilege is a passive form of active affliction. Equality and justice feel like oppression to unaware privileged people. Unaware privileged men feel oppressed when the voices of women are amplified. Unaware privileged white people feel oppressed when the causes of black people are magnified. Unaware privileged affluent people feel attacked when the plight of poor people is illuminated. Unaware privileged heterosexual people feel assaulted when the oppression of Q+ people is highlighted.

The best way I can explain this is in the conversations I have had with some Black people about addressing the way we have oppressed our Black Q+ neighbors. People conjure up the most obscure, illogical arguments for why Q+ people should not be allowed to live their lives as they are. One of my least favorite arguments is, "If gay people are allowed to freely get married then we won't be able to repopulate the earth. It takes a male and a female to procreate." This is the fallacy of conflating harm with discomfort.

Two mature, consenting adults with same-gender attraction choosing to be in a committed relationship with each other does not in any way hinder my ability to procreate with my wife. The gay couple's relationship does not change the dynamics of my heterosexual relationship. We just need to be honest that their relationships make many of us uncomfortable. But it is not the responsibility of the gay couple to carry the burden of our discomfort. We need to deal with why we are uncomfortable. If gay people were trying to demand that every human enter into a same-gender loving relationship, that would be harmful. But I have never heard of a Q+ person demanding that their orientation become the rule for everyone else. It is actually the other way around. Straight people of faith, in particular, are guilty of trying to impose our natural attractions onto our Q+ neighbors. Their natural attractions cause us discomfort. Our imposition of heteronormativity onto their lives is harmful. This is why our theological frameworks need to be based in lived experience rather than theoretical insinuations.

You may be thinking to yourself, "Well, what does the Bible say about being gay?" Great question. The problem with the question is that it is often rooted in poor biblical scholarship. Unpacking the very few (emphasis on "very few") passages in the Bible that seem to address the issue of same-gender attraction is not my assignment in this book. There is a plethora of resources that can walk you through that process. Consider reading *Changing Our Mind* by David Gushee or *Our Lives Matter* by Pamela Lightsey to further explore the biblical implications on this issue.

The second problem with that question is that it presupposes that whatever the Bible says on a matter settles the matter. Rule-keeping theological frameworks generally use "The Bible" as the standard by which our faith should be measured. Greatest Commandment Theology uses the Greatest Commandment as the standard by which our faith should be measured. To take it a step further, Greatest Commandment Theology uses the Greatest Commandment as the standard by which the relevance of the whole Bible should be measured. The major paradigm shift is to replace the question, "What does the Bible say about that?" with "How does the Greatest Commandment apply here?"

Besides, if we hearken back to the distinction between doctrine and the Bible we'll see that generally when we ask "What does the Bible say about that?" what we really mean is "What does our doctrine say about that?" Start asking the question, "How does the Greatest Commandment apply here?" Give it a try. Say it with me. "How does the Greatest Commandment apply here?" Making this shift will literally change your worldview. It will change how you see yourself, how you see other people and how you see God. It will change how you see sin, how you see love and how you see justice. It will change how you see heaven and hell. It will change how you see life in general.

Chapter 9

What does the Bible say about that?

Slavery in the Bible is a classic case of why asking "What does the Bible say about that?" is an insufficient question to settle all matters. Consulting what the Bible says about slavery is an acceptable way to begin the discussion. But it is a profoundly dangerous and harmful way to settle the discussion.

During the mid-19th century a great debate raged between defenders of slavery and abolitionists. The interesting aspect of this debate regarding the institution of slavery is that both groups used the Bible to make their arguments. As we will see, the biblical case for slavery is strong and direct. The biblical case against slavery requires principle-based implications without any direct condemnations of slavery itself.

A debate about the morality of slavery seems absurd in 2020. It is such an issue of the past that at times we may forget that, at one time, it was a real and very divisive issue. The white people of this country did not institute slavery as a rebellion against religion. They did it with biblical precedent. In the decades leading up to the American Civil War, a number of biblically based arguments were made for and against the institution of slavery. Reverend E.W. Warren of First Baptist Church of Christ in Macon, GA said the following in his 1861 sermon, "Scriptural Vindication of Slavery:"

> I may premise, that though the Revelation from heaven is given, to man as a sinner, yet it nowhere recognizes his right to sin, or regulates the manner in which he is to commit sin—but it will not be

> denied by any sane man, that ***the Bible does recognize*** the owner's right to his slave as property, and regulates the relation. Therefore slavery is not sin... ***A higher law than the Bible must be found before slavery can be condemned.***

Warren's reasoning is plausible based on the rule-keeping paradigm with which he viewed the Bible. His view suggests that the Bible references slavery in a number of instances. In none of these instances do the writers of scripture condemn slavery. If God intended for slavery to cease, would it not have been explicitly revealed somewhere in the scriptures, especially since it was so explicitly *condoned* in the scriptures? In other words, Rev. Warren's response to people who questioned slavery was, "Well, what does the Bible say about it?"

Other publications and articles shared during the 19th century claimed a biblical defense for slavery, an institution that destroyed African families, robbed a culture group of its heritage and still has repercussions well into the 21st century. One of the most noteworthy publications that laid out four basic arguments for slavery was written by Thornton Stringfellow of Richmond, VA. His four theses are as follows:

1) Slavery was divinely sanctioned among the patriarchs.

2) Slavery was incorporated into Israel's national constitution.

3) Slavery was recognized and approved by Jesus Christ and the apostles.

4) Slavery is a merciful institution.

Below is an excerpt from the publication that shares, in brief, the position of pro-slavery Christians. I added parenthetical scriptural references in case you need to fact check this information:

"We theologians and Christian statesmen from 1815 to 1865, hold that the Bible says nothing to condemn slavery as sinful, and some of us maintain that the Bible in fact commands slavery. Rooted in Noah's prophetic cursing of Ham-Canaan's descendants (Gen 9:24-27), slavery has been and should be practiced by God's people. Abraham, champion of the faith, had many slaves (Gen 12:5, 16, 24:34-35, 20:14). God told the Israelites to buy slaves and gave specific instructions pertaining to their service (Lev 25:39-46). Jesus never spoke against slavery but used the slave image as a model for Christian conduct (Luke 17:7-10). Paul (1 Tim 6:1-2) and Peter (1 Pet 2:18-20) instructed masters and slaves in how to conduct themselves as Christians, and Paul obeyed fugitive slave law in sending the runaway slave Onesimus back to Philemon, his master (Phil). Nowhere does the Bible condemn slavery. Either believe the Bible and support slavery or oppose slavery and throw out the Bible as God's authoritative Word."

During this 19th-century debate the various pro-slavery representatives used various examples from every section of the Bible argue their point. Their biblical references explicitly refer to slaves and slavery. These slaves were to be dealt with harshly when necessary. They were to suffer punishment for doing no wrong. They were considered the property of their masters and could be willed to their masters' children. Again, when confronted with the topic of abolishing slavery, they responded with the question, "Well, what does the Bible have to say about that?"

What, then, was the argument during this heated debate against the institution of slavery in America? It apparently was a powerful argument because it galvanized a nation to fight for the extermination slavery in the mid-19th century.

The anti-slavery publications of the 19th century made the same claims to scriptural appeal as did the pro-slavery arguments. Their position, in brief, suggested that "slavery is man-stealing" (Ex. 21:16). They also suggested that the release of the Israelites from Egyptian bondage implies that God hates and condemns slavery. William Ellery Channing's anti-slavery publication suggested that slavery reduces human life to property. He argued that "the injustices and cruelties of slavery fly squarely in the face of Jesus' command to love others as yourself."

The anti-slavery movement had many compelling arguments for why slavery was an unjust institution. The issue is that their biblical arguments did not disprove the arguments of the pro-slavery stance. The argument that "slavery is man-stealing" found in Exodus 21 appears just a few verses prior to instructions on the severity with which a master can beat his male or female slave without fear of punishment. The appeal to love one's neighbor as oneself is indeed a compelling argument but does not explicitly say the ownership of slaves is counter to this notion. The Bible is full of references to master/slave relationships where human life is reduced to property status.

Ultimately, this debate did not end with the abolitionists reigning victorious from an argument perspective. Slavery was not completely abolished as an institution until the end of the American Civil War, which is still, to date, the deadliest war in American history. The slavery debate was a prime factor in the Civil War. Although the South lost the Civil War, there is still no declared winner of the biblical slavery debate.

The pro-slavery debaters were correct. One more time in case you read that too fast: The PRO-SLAVERY debaters were correct. The Bible does not at any point directly condemn slavery. That was true in the 19th century and it is still true in the 21st century. Yet, one would be hard-pressed to find a significant number of Christians today who would attempt to biblically justify a shift back to chattel slavery in America.

There are no publications being released in 2020 about whether slavery is right or wrong. This goes back to the statement made by the defenders of slavery, "A higher law than the Bible must be found before slavery can be condemned." The higher law is in the Bible, but it is the standard by which the relevance of the rest of the Bible should be measured. The higher law is The Greatest Commandment. The debate of the 19th century proves that biblical appeals alone are insufficient to tear down all unjust systems of oppression, because in the case of slavery, the system of oppression was embedded into the culture in which the Bible was written.

The Bible does not say that slavery was right. The Bible does not say that slavery was wrong. And none of us can point out a text where God explicitly condemns slavery as a sin. We can find scriptures that allude to God's condemnation of slavery based on over-arching principles. But there is no text that explicitly condemns slavery. Yet, the average Christian will, without hesitation, explicitly condemn slavery on all levels as an egregious sin. If we hinge our arguments on the question, "What does the Bible say about slavery?" to resolve the matter, we will have to seriously reconsider whether slavery should have ever been abolished. But when we ask the question, "How does the Greatest Commandment apply here?" we can easily see that there is no place for slavery in humanity, regardless of what the rest of the Bible says. The question we must then ask is this:

What other harmful active afflictions have we practiced based on "what the Bible says"?

The church's mistreatment of women is supported by what the Bible says. White America's oppression of Black people is supported by what the Bible says. The church's oppression of Q+ people is supported by what the Bible says. If we want to have a holistic conversation about any of these issues, we must go beyond what the Bible says. We must ask "How does the Greatest Commandment apply here?" When we start with the Greatest Commandment, we can appreciate much of the sound wisdom we find throughout scripture. At the same time, when we start with the Greatest Commandment, we can identify the errors in scripture. The Bible is not some magic book that God dropped from the sky into our laps. The Bible is sacred, not sovereign.

Many of us take "loving our neighbor" out of context. We say that our love for our neighbor is doing everything we can to direct them towards God's will and save them from a burning hell. So, we use our understanding of scripture as an excuse for our unbridled condemnation and relentless judgement of others. And we end up making people's lives a living hell in the name of getting them into heaven. We require people to deny their own humanity. We shame people for not meeting cultural standards. And we ostracize people for thinking or believing differently. The reality is if you are going to make my life a living hell, I don't want to go to your heaven anyway.

Slapping random Bible verses on issues is an inadequate measure of sin. A responsible conversation about the nature of sin should revolve around the Greatest Commandment. The next time you think to condemn yourself or condemn someone else, ask yourself, "Am I being harmed by this action or this mindset? Are any of my neighbors being harmed by this action or mindset?" These two questions have not failed me yet.

"But Kristian, I'm still not clear on how I'm supposed to base all of my actions on The Greatest Commandment. Do you have anything else besides, 'Do no harm?'" Thanks for asking. You never cease to amaze me with your timely questions.

Chapter 10

Love in Action

The first aspect of love is "do no harm." When I am confronted with a dilemma or a difficult decision, I must ask myself "How does the Greatest Commandment apply here? Will my decision harm me? Will my decision harm my neighbor? If the answer to both of those questions is "no," then I should be confident that my decision will not cause any harm to my relationship with God. I should bear in mind that sometimes my decisions will make me and/or my neighbor uncomfortable. But sometimes discomfort is necessary.

The next aspect of love is "how can I help?" Greatest Commandment Theology calls us to harm no one and help as many people as we can, including ourselves. We should extend grace. Give respect. Buildup. Encourage. Include. Affirm. Embrace. Sometimes helping myself requires me to make my neighbor uncomfortable. Sometimes helping my neighbor requires me to make myself uncomfortable. Sometimes helping my neighbor requires me to make another neighbor uncomfortable. Loving my neighbor as myself may require me, at times, to resist the evil my neighbor inflicts upon me or another neighbor.

If we want a clear picture of how Jesus set out to execute The Greatest Commandment, consider how he introduced his ministry. In Luke 4:18-19, Jesus begins his ministry with a clear declaration:

> "The spirit of the Lord is upon me, because he has anointed me to bring good news to the poor. He

> has sent me to proclaim release to the captives and recovery of sight to the blind, to let the oppressed go free, to proclaim the year of the Lord's favor."

The preacher in me wants to unpack this statement line by line and sermonize it, but in the words of Rev. Brown from *Coming to America*, "I didn't come to preach to y'all tonight." If you don't recognize that film reference, watch *Coming to America* now!

Jesus steps onto the scene as a relative unknown. He is not yet the Jesus who has preached life-changing sermons on mountains and performed countless miracles. Here, he is simply introducing himself to his audience. He wants people to know his endgame before he officially gets started. He starts his ministry by declaring, in no uncertain terms, that he is focused on the poor, the prisoner, the sick and the oppressed. Based on some of the rule-keeping doctrines many of us practice, you would think that Jesus' mission was to stop people from having sex, dancing, drinking, smoking, cussing, being gay and skipping church.

For those of us who call ourselves Christians, what we are saying is that we have committed ourselves to following the way of Christ. His primary focus should therefore be our primary focus. Sure, we must consider the context of his life because, remember, if you take a text out of its context, all you have left is a con. But if you recall the sermons most of us hear in our churches, they have very little to do with the poor, the prisoner, the sick and the oppressed.

We talk more about people getting delivered from going to nightclubs than we talk about reducing recidivism and helping restore voting rights to felons who have served their time. Jesus did say, "Release to the captives," after all. In our context that implies more than simply getting people out of physical prisons. Our country has a criminal justice system that imprisons people even after they are "released" back into the civilian population. (To read more about how this system functions read *The New Jim Crow* by Michelle Alexander.)

Jesus approaches his ministry much like a good entrepreneur approaches their business. Every business needs to have a vision statement and a mission statement. The problem is that most people, including most entrepreneurs, don't know the difference between the two.

Your vision statement declares where you hope to ultimately see yourself and how you want people in the market to see you in the future. My vision statement for my clothing business, P-Squared Custom Clothiers, is to be seen as the industry's most trusted wardrobe consultants.

A mission statement articulates how you plan to achieve your vision statement. My company's mission statement is to optimize each client's professional image through impeccable customer service, custom clothing, and professional image consulting. My mission helps me to achieve my vision.

Jesus' vision for his people is that we love God in how we love our neighbor, which reflects the love we have for ourselves. He helps us understand how to achieve that vision by giving us his mission statement, that we fight for and advocate on the behalf of the poor, prisoner, sick and oppressed.

We should never overlook the reality that sometimes we have to fight for ourselves when we are the poor, the prisoner, the sick and the oppressed. In identifying our place in these categories, we must discern whether we are being harmed or if we are merely uncomfortable. Jesus's mission statement is not focused on us obtaining, in the words of E.

Dewey Smith, more cash, cars, clothes and creature comforts. It challenges us to look at those among us who are hurting. It challenges us to honestly ask ourselves are we the cause of this pain. It then challenges us to do what we can to help them. Sometimes that requires us to recognize that we have some bad neighbors who are actively afflicting us for the sake of their own comfort. Once we recognize these bad neighbors, we need to resist them in order for us to be whole at the expense of their comfort. The Greatest Commandment calls us to comfort the afflicted even if it means afflicting the comfortable. Sometimes, my privilege makes me the comfortable one that needs to be afflicted.

Jesus' mission statement calls upon Jesus' followers to disrupt injustice when we encounter it. Jesus was the ultimate disrupter. During his ministry he completely disrupted how people interpreted the scriptures. He disrupted social norms by associating with societal outcasts. He disrupted people's expectations when he came as a peaceful prophet messiah instead of a warrior messiah. He saved us by dying as a victim of violence rather than initiating violence like some of his predecessors. Jesus is an example that love in action often requires disruption.

The Audacity of Disruption

An interesting story about the audacity of disruption features Moses in Exodus 2. Moses was born in a volatile time in the life of the Hebrew people. They were slaves in Egypt and Pharaoh had just issued an edict that all newborn Hebrew boys were to be killed. Moses' mom, Jochebed, was pretty brilliant though. She concocted a plan to save Moses' life. She ultimately worked it out where Moses was raised in Pharaoh's palace by Pharaoh's daughter. To top it off, Pharaoh's daughter paid Jochebed to nurse Moses for her. In other words, she went from the fear that her son might be murdered by Pharaoh's followers, to having Pharaoh's daughter pay her to nurse her own son. That is legendary.

Although Moses had the privilege of being raised by Pharaoh's daughter in Pharaoh's palace, he always had a heart for his Hebrew people. One day, he saw an Egyptian soldier brutalizing one of his Hebrew brothers and in an attempt to defend his Hebrew brother, he killed the Egyptian soldier. When Pharaoh found out what Moses did, he sought to kill Moses. So Moses had to flee Egypt.

He eventually settled in Midian, where he encountered seven Midian sisters who came to a well to draw water for their father's flocks. But some shepherds drove away the sisters before they could draw the water.

Moses arrived in Midian as a fugitive. He was subject to the oppressive regime of a blood-thirsty Pharaoh who wanted to kill him. He was in a new country where he didn't know anybody. (I imagine he had a lot on his mind.) He also realized that these women needed some help. He lived in a culture where women were a subclass; in many instances they were treated as property. The moral of the story is this: Even with all the challenges that Moses faced, he still recognized he could be oppressed and privileged at the same time.

This lesson held true in Moses' day and it still rings true today. Greatest Commandment Theology challenges us to see how we need to care for ourselves, and how we also need to care for others. Moses had to run to save his own life. But he didn't turn off his compassion for other people who didn't enjoy the privileges he had. He was a fugitive *and* he was a man in a patriarchal society. In this story, he shows how oppression and privilege can be held in tension with each other.

At the time I'm writing this, my culture is not as patriarchal as Moses', but we are still very much a patriarchal society. We've never elected a woman to serve as President or Vice-President of our country. And many of our churches have never and would never imagine calling a woman to pastor them. Women are paid less in the workplace on average for the same jobs that men do. Statistics suggest that 1 out of 3 women have been subjected to some sort of sexual abuse.

It is possible for me, as a Black man, oppressed in a white supremacist society, to also acknowledge that there is work I must do to combat the injustices women face. Greatest Commandment Theology calls us to acknowledge that we can be oppressed and privileged at the same time.

Back to the story. When Moses saw the shepherds run off the seven sisters from the well, he jumped into action, fought off the shepherds and helped the sisters water their father's flock. The text actually reads in the New Revised Standard Version that Moses "got up and came to their defense." He didn't merely acknowledge his privilege; he was responsible with it. He lived out the Greatest Commandment in this moment by recognizing that advocacy requires action.

If I love you, I see you being mistreated, and it is in my power to do something about it, I need to get up and come to your defense. It is really that simple. When Moses saw injustice, he got up and he came. Many of us, when we see injustice, tend to sit back and watch. The Greatest Commandment requires more of us. It requires action. This will look different depending on the context.

As I write this book, protests are taking place all over the world in support of black people brutalized by law enforcement. There are more white people than black people at some of these protests. That is advocacy in action.

But going to a protest is not the only way to advocate for people. The Greatest Commandment allows for us to love with whatever actions fit our context. It may mean going to a protest or signing petitions or contacting political representatives or organizing movements or donating money or organizing educational efforts or any combination of these. In the words of my friend, Dr. Greg DeLoach, "Some of us need to take a knee. Some of us need to take a stand. Some of us need to step aside. But all of us need to move. It's not enough to say we are sorry if we're not moving if we're not doing something."

The point is that Moses got up and came to their defense. He acted. Loving our neighbors as ourselves requires us to act. Remember, the baseline requirement of love is to do no harm. As we grow in our love for our neighbors, we need to start asking ourselves, How can we help?

Back to the story one more time as I head to my seat (You've probably heard this from a Black preacher a million times. Which means you also know we almost never head to our seats after the first time we promise we will. But I promise this is my last point.) This part of the Moses story tripped me out: When the sisters returned home, their father said to them, "How is it that you have come back so soon today?" The implications of this question are sobering to say the least.

These sisters went out to fill their troughs with water at the well and water their father's flock. That's it. That's all. Instead, they were met with oppressive shepherds who drove them away, upending the entire flow of their process. Then Moses jumps in and fights off the shepherds by himself and helps the sisters with their duties. At least to me, it seems that this would have slowed down their routine. It would make more sense to me if when they returned home their father said, "What took you all so long? I was worried sick!" No, that's not what he said. After the disturbance they experienced, their father asked, "How is it that you have come back so soon today?"

Could it be that these sisters had to fight off shepherds by themselves every day? Could it be that oppression was a part of their daily routine? Could it be that brutality was their norm? Could it be that Moses steps in to disrupt the normalcy of their oppression?

Sometimes, when we are detached from another person's struggle, we assume that their mistreatment is an isolated incident. It happens every time a police officer brutalizes a black person on camera. White people, in particular, write it off as one bad cop. And when it happens on camera the next week, they write it off again as an isolated incident. And when it happens two days later, they write it off again as yet, one more isolated incident. Dammit, at some point we need to recognize that people are in a pattern of oppression!

Living out the Greatest Commandment means disrupting the normalcy of oppression people experience on a regular basis. When Jesus said, "the poor will always be with you," he was not stating an ideal outcome. He was saying the poor will always be among you because there will always be people in power who insist on keeping others in poverty. I write prophetically when I say that the oppressed, the brutalized, and the traumatized will always be among us. Greatest Commandment Theology challenges us to ensure there are less oppressed, brutalized, and traumatized people when we leave here than when we arrived.

Greatest Commandment Theology calls us to change the world one person at a time. Every time we leverage our privilege in spite of our oppression, we have changed the world. Every time we get up and come to another's defense, we have changed the world. Every time we disrupt the normalcy of someone's oppression, even when that oppression is our own, we have changed the world.

If you want to know what Greatest Commandment Theology looks like in action, it looks like justice. Since we are all so obsessed with what the afterlife may look like, when Jesus addresses the end times in Matthew 25, he says that all of the nations will be gathered before him. Not the Christian nations. Not the Baptist nations. Not the Apostolic nations. Not the Methodist nations. Not the Catholic nations. Not the Western nations. Not the Episcopal Nations. ALL THE NATIONS will be gathered before him. Jesus says there will be a separation of people who represent all the nations based on some criteria.

Based on our rule-keeping theological paradigms we might assume that Jesus would separate people based on who went to church the most and who prayed the most and who gave the most in the offering and who read their Bibles the most. We would assume that Jesus would separate people based on who cussed the least; the people who didn't drink and smoke; the people who had the least sex outside of marriage; and the people who didn't live a gay lifestyle.

But that's not what Jesus said. He said to the people whom he deemed to be righteous, "I was hungry, and you fed me. I was thirsty, and you gave me something to drink. I was a stranger, and you welcomed me. I was naked, and you gave me clothing. I was sick, and you took care of me. I was in prison, and you visited me." And when the people Jesus deems righteous say, "When did we do these things?" Jesus will respond and say, "Truly I tell you, just as you did it to one of the least of these who are members of my family, you did it to me."

This kind of righteousness requires a deep love for oneself that can then be projected onto those around us. This kind of righteousness recognizes I can't help everybody, but I refuse to actively afflict anybody. This kind of righteousness says, "When I am in position to help someone who is in need, I will get up and come to their defense." Greatest Commandment Theology prioritizes these words from Dr. Cornel West, "Never forget that justice is what love looks like in public." Greatest Commandment Theology challenges us to break the rules if it means someone's life will be made better.

Chapter 11

Mama's Story

I talk a lot about my dad because I inherited so many of his characteristics. In my experience, kids in two-parent households are generally drawn to one parent more than the other. Based on how much I talk about my dad you probably wouldn't know that I am a mama's boy just as much as I am my daddy's son. My mom has always been my biggest supporter, even when my dad was unnecessarily hard on me. However, I must admit that, as the baby brother, I was the beneficiary of the parenting lessons my mom and dad learned while practicing on my two older siblings. My dad was much more mellow by the time I reached my pre-teen years. (This is what I call Baby Privilege.) When my dad died in 2010, the bond between my mom and me became even stronger.

When I started the small group in 2015 that would eventually become The Faith Community, my mom was right there to support me. I believe she was looking for a place of spiritual connection just as much as she was looking for a way to support her son. She had been somewhat of a church outsider since my father passed. No place she went truly felt like home. It would make sense, then, that she would naturally feel at home in her own son's ministry, right? Not so much.

I started the small group on the premise of Greatest Commandment Theology which, inevitably, includes the practice of Bible Criticism. As I see it, to take the Bible seriously, we need to consult it critically. And I take the Bible way too seriously to always read it literally. We need to ask questions of the Bible. We need to push back at times. When we read troubling passages, we need to ask, "How does the Greatest Commandment apply here?" This approach to "Bible Study" was jarring for my mom. Much like many of our parents, she raised me in the rule-keeping theological framework.

The biblical truths and doctrinal concepts we were unpacking in our small group seemed heretical to her. Mom had spent 60 years in the same theological framework. Greatest Commandment Theology was sensible and scary to her at the same time. Sometimes it was the sensibility of it that made it scary.

In one small group we unpacked the problems with the story in which Samuel tells Saul to kill all the Amalekites. Mom said she always had internal questions about that story but she would just suppress them. Many people suppress their valid questions using the wisdom of Proverbs 3:5-6 which says, "Trust in the Lord with all your heart, and do not rely on your own insight. In all of your ways acknowledge him, and he will make straight your paths." This proverb provides great wisdom for us when we encounter issues, we can neither explain nor understand. This proverb is problematic when we apply it to a biblical concept that we know is counter to the Greatest Commandment. We don't need to throw out our common sense for the sake of maintaining the divine status of the Bible. Because of the pressures placed upon her by her religious culture, Mom had been suppressing questions and concerns for most of her life. Participating in my ministry opened up Pandora's Box. And it was uncomfortable.

I know Mom well, so I can feel it when her energy changes. I know when she's upset or angry or unsettled. There were a couple of sessions which shook Mom to her core. I remember I called her after one of our small groups to check in and she told me, "Son, I don't know if I can be a part of this. It's too much. I feel like everything I once knew is being stripped away from me and I am starting over from scratch."

Bear in mind: Mom isn't a novice. She was a seminary-trained Minister of Christian Education at our church when I was growing up. That just goes to show how deeply embedded her theology was. And she was ready to walk away from her own son's ministry when she didn't have a viable back-up plan. She didn't feel at home anywhere else, but Greatest Commandment Theology made her feel insecure in everything she thought she knew about the Bible. She loved the freedom of being able to question the scriptures that gave her pause. But she was overwhelmed when others questioned the concepts that she assumed needed no critique.

Many of you who read this book and decided to explore the Greatest Commandment Theology framework may have a similar experience to my mom. At times it will be unsettling. It will be jarring. It will make you reassess a lot of the concepts you once believed. It will make you feel like you wasted too much time in your life making unnecessary sacrifices you thought brought you closer to God. You'll find yourself asking, "Well, what have I been doing all this stuff for?" It will feel like you've been cheated out of something. You may feel exposed. You may feel isolated. You may feel like you have hit a wall in your faith. That's how I felt as I began my theological evolution. And that's how mom felt when she began hers.

I am paraphrasing the 20th-century theologian Paul Tillich when I say this: Don't confuse firm beliefs with deep faith. Our unwillingness to change our beliefs is not what makes our faith strong. It just makes our faith stiff. The more stiff our faith is, the more likely it is to snap under the pressure of questioning and critique. Our faith is strengthened when we allow for some flexibility and fluidity in our beliefs. Our faith is made stronger when we recognize there are very few absolute truths in life. The only non-negotiable in Greatest Commandment Theology is that we should not engage in any mindset or activity that contradicts our love for God in how we love our neighbor as a reflection of our love for ourselves. Everything else is up for discussion. You can't simply slap a Bible verse on an issue to end the conversation. The Bible verse merely starts the conversation. In Greatest Commandment Theology we wrestle with the scriptures in community. We discern together what we believe. We identify the differences and similarities between what the writers of scripture wrote on behalf of God and what we believe we hear God saying to us today.

I'm pleased to say that Mom didn't leave the group. She pressed through her discomfort and anxiety. As exposed as she felt at times, she couldn't escape the logic of it all. It was uncomfortable for her, but it just made sense. It was counterintuitive to her embedded theology, but it just made sense. It brought up questions she never realized she had, but it just made sense. Her evolution over the past five years has inspired me.

We recently had a session at The Faith Community where we talked about a highly controversial topic. (To be fair, this describes almost every session at The Faith Community.) I checked in with her out of concern, because, just a couple of years ago that same topic would have unsettled her to the point of no return.

I said, "Mom, are you good?"

She said, "What do you mean?"

I said, "Today's session was pretty heavy. I know how some of these topics can be uncomfortable to unpack."

She replied, "Oh! No, I'm fine. That doesn't bother me anymore. I'm secure in what I know. And I'm comfortable with what I don't know."

In the wise words of the problematic historical figure Mark Twain, "It's not what you don't know that gets you into trouble. It's what you know for sure that just ain't so." Greatest Commandment Theology will teach you some new concepts and it will require you to unlearn some old concepts. When in doubt, just ask the question, "How does the Greatest Commandment apply here?"

CPSIA information can be obtained
at www.ICGtesting.com
Printed in the USA
FSHW021822280820

9 781951 472627